UNSCHOOLING

A Lifestyle of Learning

Sara McGrath

♡

With gratitude for
Maia, Ilana, and Kalea.
To borrow Ilana's words, "I'm glad that you exist."
♡
In loving memory of
Trixie, Hannah, Sinopa, Kuruk, Ahote, Kaia, and Ivan Pi-Chai
"Bubba," my other kids.

ISBN   1453866302
EAN-13   978-1453866306

Edition 4

The Unschooling Happiness Project
http://unschoolinglifestyle.com

Other books by Sara McGrath:

The Unschooling Happiness Project
a guide and memoir

Recordkeeping for Unschoolers
a spiral-bound journal

Write a Novel in 30 Days

Strange Little Girl: Memoirs of a Sad-Eyed Lady

Contents

Introduction

People who feel drawn to the philosophical ideals of unschooling often ask how to unschool. With this book, I intend to present a practical handbook for learning without school. While acknowledging that each family approaches the unschooling lifestyle from a unique standpoint, I offer the details of my family's experiences, along with specific advice for meeting legal requirements without sacrificing your ideals.

The print-on-demand model of publication makes possible continuous revision, of which I take full advantage. This book presently exists in its ~~third~~ 4th major incarnation. As with my life, I have many ideas for re*vision*ing.

> You can find a directory of my articles and other Internet sources at the companion website:
>
> The Unschooling Happiness Project
> *http://unschoolinglifestyle.com*

About Unschooling

The word 'unschooling' often confuses people, because it presents somewhat of a misnomer. People typically associate schooling with learning or education, thus follows the assumption that *un*schooling implies *un*learning or *un*educating.

However, let's make clear that *un*schooling does not imply *un*learning or *un*educating. It simply describes living without the limitations of school. So let's imagine a life of *un*limited possibilities!

In the absence of school, what do children do? They play. They do what brings them joy. They do what calls to them. They do what they need to do to get from point A to point B, learning *useful* skills along the way.

While 'unschooling' literally means 'not schooling.' This literal translation does little to explain what unschooling really looks like or feels like. Perhaps, because the term begins with a negative prefix, unschoolers typically attempt to define unschooling by what it excludes. The lack of a positive definition contributes to a multitude of misperceptions about the relationship between unschooling children and their parents.

John Holt, the school reformer turned homeschooling advocate who coined the term, did so in opposition to schooling (i.e., coercive teaching, rewards and punishments, compulsory learning, grades, tests, subjects, etc.) Unschooling, then, didn't refer to any type of schooling. It referred to something else entirely. In simplest terms, you take the schooling out of life and leave everything else. That sounds easy enough, right?

Really, unschooling means so much more than a hands-on, child-directed, experience-based, etc., way of learning. It doesn't describe a specific alternative to schooling. It just gets schooling out of the way so various unique dynamic personal creative ways of growing up, living, participating, and contributing to communities can develop.

Some unschoolers, myself included, prefer to use the term 'life learners,' instead of unschoolers. For the

> An alternative term: *life learning.*

purposes of this book, however, I have largely chosen to use the more common, original term. On the other hand, you could choose to perceive *un*schooling as *un*limiting the possibilities, which feels like a celebration of freedom.

The unschooling approach to learning things describes the way we learn naturally when left to pursue our own personal interests. As unschoolers, we *own* our interests–our passions, dreams, and goals–and also the *respons*ibility for pursuing and attaining them. We respond to our desires and go after our dreams with enthusiasm.

Fundamental to the unschooling approach, we acknowledge that

- We learn all the time;
- All learning has value; and
- We learn best by our own motivation, in our own ways.

Unschooling parents trust their children to learn what they personally need to learn. Coercion has no place in unschooling practice. If, for example, one of my daughters

> Coercive teaching strategies can harm and inhibit a child's natural curiosity and love of learning.

resists learning a skill, such as reading, I will not push her with bribes, threats, or other forms of coercion.

…Which does not mean that I will not actively help her learn to read. I will remain willing, available, and alert to what may have triggered her resistance.

The multitude of ways unschooling parents might help children learn things includes

- Introducing new topics,
- Sharing with and helping children to seek knowledge,
- Initiating and participating in learning activities, and
- Providing guidance and instruction.

Unschooling parents have many of the same concerns and hopes for their children as any parent. ♡ The differences between unschooling and more conventional approaches to homeschooling and parenting exist in philosophy rather than in practice. By outside observation, the activities of an unschooling family may appear similar to those of a more conventional homeschooling family, or they may not. Nonetheless, they will most likely *feel* different. *Un*schooling life feels joyful. A self-motivated, passion and purpose-driven life feels intrinsically right.

The unschooling lifestyle prompts us to question the true, heartfelt best interests of our children and ourselves, and to embrace our true joy-seeking natures. The unschooling lifestyle encourages us to actively maintain a respectful, mindful attitude in our interactions with others and in all that we do.

In the case of my family, the unschooling path has guided us to make a priority of actively seeking a fulfilling, happy life in addition to more conventional parenting goals.

> "Living is learning and when kids are living fully and energetically and happily they are learning a lot, even if we don't always know what it is."
> –John Holt, *A Life Worth Living* (1971)
> *http://www.holtgws.com*

About Me and My Family

During the first grade, my teachers labeled me as talented and gifted (TAG). I, along with a relatively select few other chosen six-year-olds, got to leave my regular classroom to do hands-on experiments in the TAG room. Although I felt 'special' (singled out), I didn't understand why all the kids at school didn't get to mix baking soda and vinegar or dissect clams. I didn't feel any smarter than anyone else. In retrospect, I suppose limited funding for supplies probably created the need to rank the children into academic castes.

Through perfectionism, driven by anxiety about

maintaining my elevated status, I remained in the talented or 'honors' programs throughout my school years. However, I resented time spent in school, indoors all day and under strict control. By tenth grade, I barely attended classes, preferring instead to jump on my friend's trampoline, climb at the rock quarry, or bike in the mountains. Nonetheless, I maintained high grades by dodging school guards, following class syllabi, and turning in homework and extra credit assignments.

Each quarter, I met with the school guidance counselor to discuss my increasing truancy. He noted my perfect grades and told me that he had seen this phenomenon before. He recommended that I leave high school and enter college. I took his advice, for a change of scenery and in hope of receiving adult-like (respectful) treatment. I easily passed the placement tests without preparation and began a path lacking direction or purpose other than to finally reach adult status when I could finally just live.

My husband enjoyed school. He enjoyed it all the way through graduate school during which he considered a career as a research professor. Whereas the unschooling philosophy immediately clicked for me, my husband needed more time to decide how he felt about it. By the time our first daughter reached school age, after watching her learn naturally for years, he decided firmly in favor of unschooling.

Our three daughters have never attended school. You will find examples of their daily lives and their learning adventures throughout the following pages.

An Interview with My Daughter, Maia

Let me introduce almost-eight-year-old Maia, a Seattle area resident whose family practices "radical unschooling" (a.k.a. "whole life learning.")

No Assignments. Lots of learning activities.

Maia has never attended school. That means her almost eight years have been filled with nothing but play (video games and junk food), right? Which means that she probably can't read or add two numbers together (not to mention her unavoidable social awkwardness from so little interaction), right? I asked her to comment on this.

"Um, actually, no," Maia said. "I'm very friendly. Sometimes my dance instructor asks me to stop talking so much, because we need to focus. Our recital--this is my third one--is next Saturday. Over the summer, I'm going to make friendship bracelets for all the girls in my class."

Maia has been taking structured classes, including dance and art, since she was five. She also participates in clubs and events with two local homeschooling groups, one all-inclusive and one specifically for unschoolers. At home, she likes to "do whatever I want," which includes worksheets, science projects, crafts, and a host of explicitly educational activities.

Maia started reading at age five. "I'm reading Book 2 in the Avalon series," she said. "I finished the first one when I was six." Those are 200-page books targeted at 9-12 year olds. "I read a lot," Maia said. "Sometimes I read the Civipedia for hours, because I'm interested in rulers and ancient times and mythology." Her favorite skill is math.

Video games? Yes, those, too. "I love video games and online virtual worlds," Maia said. "I just started playing Planet Orange to learn about financial literacy."

Video games and websites provided Maia's most significant motivation for learning to read. Some days she spends several hours on the Internet. Other days she likes to work in her garden, dig in the mud, and observe the natural world.

Social interactions? Maia plays with her two sisters every day, her eight-year-old neighbor (as soon as he finishes his homework) most afternoons, and her play group which meets at the river beach every Friday after art class. She also knows and exchanges pleasantries with the staff people at the post office, grocery store, library, and various other places her family goes often for routine errands.

When she grows up, Maia wants to work as 'a marine biologist for the first half of the day and a paleontologist for the second half of the day." She's preparing for that work now. In an essay she wrote: "I watch documentaries and read websites about my interests so I will be more prepared and know more when I grow up."

What about college? She plans to pursue a degree in marine biology. But before that, she has her sights set on camps, workshops, and a teen volunteer position at the Seattle Aquarium.

No rules. Lots of guidance.

I've known Maia all her life, because I'm her mother. My relationship with Maia is a partnership and a friendship. I don't tell her what to do and I don't expect her to respect or obey me. I strive to be a person she will respect. I offer experiences and help her make choices. She looks to me as a "natural authority," because I have decades of life experience that can help her understand things and reach her goals.

I share with Maia (and my other children) the principles behind common rules so she can think more deeply about life. We have an ongoing conversation about all aspects of life, emotions, social customs, etc. I see Maia as a whole person now rather an incomplete adult or an adult-in-training. Her interests and pursuits now have value and meaning beyond how they might serve her in the future.

About Communication

In an unschooling family, everyone unschools, or 'lives without school.' Everyone, including the parents, pursues their own interests. Each family member has special interests that express the unique and common aspects of their personalities and influences the dynamic of the family group.

I tend to listen more than I talk, yet I feel compelled to

share the things that bring me and my family joy. I don't like to argue, so I don't typically pit the unschooling lifestyle against other ways. I enjoy sharing with receptive people to whom unschooling might appeal if they knew about it. I feel lucky to have heard about unschooling before my children reached school age and I feel grateful to the people who spoke up and shared their experiences and wisdom.

I have a strong interest in language and communication, English-Prime (E-Prime) in particular, and also Nonviolent Communication (NVC) and compassionate communication, in general. I have largely used E-Prime to write this book. Have you noticed? I hope not.

With the intent of improving clarity, directness, and honesty, E-Prime simplifies the English language by omitting the verb 'to be,' along with its conjugates (i.e., am, are, is, was, were, been, being.) 'Be,' which does not exist in all languages (i.e., Lakota-Dakota), promotes passive, ambiguous language that can confuse or mislead recipients who have sensitivity to subtle judgments or untruths.

> Language influences perception.

For example, compare the following. "E-Prime is best." E-Prime translation: "I prefer to use E-Prime." The tool of E-Prime language helps us take responsibility for actions or ideas. It clearly attributes who did it with what they did or thought or felt, etc. It promotes active voice, honest, clear, nonjudgmental communication. E-Prime requires the speaker to think carefully before putting thoughts into words.

> "To exist or not to exist? I ask this question."
> –Translated *Hamlet*

Even though we may know that a speaker communicates from a personal, opinion-based perspective, some people still respond defensively when they hear an opinion worded as a fact, implied by a 'to be' verb. E-Prime aids peaceful communication.

To Clarify My Meaning:

"I am an unschooler" translates to "I unschool" or "I learn through life experiences."

"Unschooling is great!" translates to "Unschooling works for me" or "I enjoy unschooling" or "I prefer unschooling."

"Just be" translates to "Just do" or "Just relax," "Just exist," "Focus on your breath," or "Enjoy the moment."

In other words, think more deeply about what you truly want to say.

Some people don't notice the difference between 'to be' language and E-Prime. I do, so I use it. You may catch me using the word 'because,' a compound of 'cause to be,' because I have not yet found an alternative (i.e., 'for the reason that...') which does not result in a tongue tripping, cumbersome sentence, and also because, in common usage, it doesn't always translate literally as 'cause to be.' Sometimes I slip up and use a 'to be' verb out of habit.

My efforts toward self-improvement continue ever onward, learning and unlearning and learning anew. Just when I think I have arrived at my fully enlightened destination, I encounter a new challenge and begin the cycle again, which keeps life interesting

About Behavior & Temperament

I have heard suggested that parents drawn to unschooling must surely have calm and easy-going personalities. That gave me pause. While I may appear patient or relaxed as compared to some parents, truly my behavior patterns have grown from a controlling, perfectionistic, high-strung personality to a manner that feels a lot better and continues to get more positive and joyful every day.

During early motherhood, I quickly realized that I had a

choice before me. I could fight to master my little daughter's fiery will, standing in her way until she backed down, coercing or forcing my will upon her, or I could get creative and seek out a way to meet both our needs and live the happier, more loving and respectful life together which I truly wanted.

I questioned a lot of 'the way things are done' in those days and I have experienced many shifts over the years that continue to bring joy and contentment into my life and the lives of my children, which my past personality would not have thought possible.

I didn't gravitate toward unschooling because I already had a calm and easy-going nature. I reached for it because I wanted that peace and calm in my life.

Natural Learning

Unschoolers often use terms such as self-directed, interest-driven, delight-driven, whole life (holistic), and natural learning to refer to the unschooling style of learning.

Unschooling provides a varied and flexible approach to experiencing and learning new things which predates the establishment of conventional schooling methodology. It often puts conventional methods to friendlier uses and embraces new technologies. This chapter includes sections on

> Mohandas Gandhi once said something to the effect of *"One should not confuse the habitual with the natural."* We can easily apply this sentiment the way we help children learn.

- Play,
- Anarchy,
- Teaching,
- Early academics,
- Learning styles,
- Action styles, and
- Homeschooling styles.

By whatever name we call unschooling, it describes an approach to living with children in which a family lives and learns together in respectful partnership. Many unschooling families come from a natural, responsive, 'attachment parenting' style of living with children.

Some people refer to unschooling as natural learning, because it often manifests as a variety of learning practices that predate the invention of conventional schooling methods.

These natural practices may include trial, observation, invention, asking for instruction, or any other activity that occurs naturally to the learner as a way to accomplish personal goals.

Although the term, *natural*, may not evoke the image of a child using modern technology, such as computers, television, etc., these tools can fit within a natural learning style.

Attachment Parenting & The Continuum Concept

In general, the 'attachment parenting' approach to raising children includes practices that demonstrate awareness of and responsiveness to a young child's needs. This awareness and responsiveness relies on a strong, foundational bond between mother and baby, followed by other close relationships.

Dr. William Sears, who coined the term (*The Attachment Parenting Book*. Little, Brown and Company, 2001), listed seven fundamental practices, or 'attachment tools' for developing and supporting an attached relationship between caregiver and child.

- Birth bonding
- Breastfeeding
- Babywearing
- Bedding close to baby (cosleeping)
- Belief in baby's cries as communication
- Beware of baby trainers (experts, methods)
- Balance between needs of caregiver and child

In her book, *The Continuum Concept* (Da Capo Press, 1986), Jean Liedloff described a peaceful way of living with children, observed during her time with an indigenous South American people. She proposed that all babies have instinctual expectations of reliable, responsive care, including an in-arms period (babywearing), breastfeeding on-cue, a family bed (cosleeping), etc.

She further proposed that when caregivers consistently ignore babies, the babies learn to disregard their own needs and sense of worth, and that toddler tantrums, considered normal in Western cultures, result from confusion and frustration from not experiencing the natural human expectations for love and freedom.

The Importance of Play

You can feel the joyous and abundant energy present in the state of play. Playing creates an altered state in which the mind opens to new possibilities. Children instinctually jump and move their bodies, touch and manipulate things, engage others in silliness and friendly competition, make noise, and imagine stories.

Play may include fantasy, make-believe, poetry, song, drama, art, and on and on. Children use these activities to explore and understand the world, to make meaningful and useful discoveries.

Young children engaged in self-motivated activities learn a multitude of concepts in a natural, informal, and enjoyable way. For example, very young children learn to walk and talk, count and identify symbols, differentiate between light, dark, and various colors, observe the natural world and social relationships, and feel the effects of motion, gravity, etc., with little or no explicit instruction.

Children likewise continue to learn through playing, having fun, experimenting, etc., for as long as they remain free

> Unschooling parents take play seriously.

from a coercive teaching environment. Coercive pressure, based in fear, blocks successful, joyful learning.

You may have heard that learning and fun don't go together or that learning is not all fun and games, but unschoolers challenge this precept. We assert that
- Play provides a perfectly valid mode of learning; and
- Effective learning need not cause difficultly or

unpleasantness.

> Everyone needs play.
> National Institute for Play
> *http://www.nifplay.org*

Unschooling and Anarchy

Some people fear that unschooling will promote anarchy, by which they mean 'chaos, lawlessness, and disorder.' However, like the 'un' in unschooling, the 'an' in anarchy, simply means 'without a ruler.' As with unschooling, people often misunderstand the concept of anarchy.

Anarchy describes, not the absence of order, but the absence of rule, i.e., coercive authority and strict top-down

> A true leader has natural authority.

hierarchical organization. Anarchy describes a community of cooperative partnerships, responsible self-governance, and voluntary, respectful relationships between leaders and followers. In an anarchist community, leaders gain followers through natural authority, i.e, useful skills and experience.

A ruler, on the other hand, such as an authoritarian parent, uses laws, enforcement, and punishments to create an involuntary ruler-follower relationship. Therefore, the ruler does not truly lead.

Unschooling parents use their natural authority as experienced elders to help their children achieve personal goals, but also remain willing to follow the child's lead when it makes sense to do so. In this way, children and parents live cooperatively in partnership.

According to anarchist philosophy, parents have *respons*ibility for and to their children, but not

ownership of them. For example, my responsiveness to my children, the reliable and loving meeting of their needs, creates the foundation from which they mature into cooperative, free-thinking people, unbound by unmet needs. We learn respectful cooperation by experiencing it.

Anarchist philosophy views education as inseparable from life itself, and discipline as the development of self-regulation which can only come from a life free of inhibition, threat, and coercion. Unschooling parents guide their children by acting in a thoughtful, responsible, and courteous manner.

If one of my children acts in a way that endangers her or someone else, I respond by protecting whomever needs protection. I may offer empathy and engage the offending child in conversation about the incident to help the child understand the feelings involved, but I will not attempt to add pain (where pain already exists) through arbitrary punishment.

Teaching

Unschoolers typically avoid the word *teach* to avoid its association with coercive teaching methods and because many don't believe that the phenomenon of teaching exists. Some languages don't have a word for it. In English, the word *teach* describes an act done by a teacher to a student, which causes the student to learn something.

Unschooling philosophy holds that learning happens within the learner through the learner's efforts. For example, each of my children learned to use eating utensils, walk, and talk through a natural desire and compulsion to master these useful skills. My actions may have helped them learn, but I didn't cause the learning. I didn't teach.

The learner actively undertakes learning rather than passively receives information or instruction from a teacher. An unschooling parent does not to teach, but helps children learn.

I sometimes use the word *teach*–translation: help learn–with a noncoercive slant to the meaning. You can boycott the word *teach*, or you can reclaim it for your own uses, as you desire. I have chosen to remake the word in my own image.

Unschooling parents respect and celebrate the variety of ways children learn naturally. We trust that children want to learn. They have no need of coercion masquerading as encouragement, incentive, or any other external motivation.

Children naturally rebel against coercive teaching. Coercion disrespects the child and can harm the child's self-confidence. In other words, coercion disregards the child's feelings and needs.

As social creatures, we never require coercion (i.e., threats, pressure, material incentives) to inspire us to want to fit in. We naturally want to connect and join in community. We want to contribute and play an important role. We want to learn useful skills (i.e., reading, writing, math, scientific observation and measurement, etc.), because we need those tools to navigate the world.

My husband uses advanced math and scientific concepts on a daily basis. I don't. If I needed those skills, I would learn them. If my children need those skills, they will learn them.

Unschooling parents trust that their children will seek out these skills when they need them. However, unschooling parents don't necessarily wait for their children to specifically request information or guidance regarding a particular skill. A parent might offer help or new information at any time.

We all learn by exploring, trying things, asking questions, and asking for help when we need it.

New unschooling parents sometimes hesitate to initiate

conversations or activities which resemble teaching. However, unschooling philosophy fully supports any interaction with interested and receptive children, i.e, demonstration, instruction, etc.

Outwardly, this may look like a lecture or a homework assignment, but the unschooling activity will lack any coercive or mandatory element. As long as our children agree to participate, we can share with them all that we know and help them find the answers to any questions for which we don't have ready answers. If we already knew all the answers, we would miss out on many mystery solving and treasure seeking adventures.

As social creatures, we desire to belong and contribute to our communities. We accomplish this by learning all that we can about the people and the world around us. If we remain available to our children, spend a lot of time with them, and have fun together, they will feel safe and confident enough to step out into the world to learn even more.

Early Academics

Young children crave and need direct interaction with the physical world. That means generous amounts of freedom to touch, taste, smell, listen, and watch. Free play introduces the child to scientific observation (a.k.a. curiosity and exploration).

From a desire to give children an early advantage, parents may make the mistake of focusing on abstract academic subjects before a young child has had sufficient experience exploring the concrete, physical world, and absorbing concepts through immersion.

Children learn math and reading, for example, in stages. They traverse a hierarchy of understanding. For

> In a literate society, a child cannot fail to notice letters and numbers. Children want to understand them.

example, a very young child, rapidly learning to communicate, will develop awareness of numeric and alphabetic symbols. This may happen while a parent reads to the child, while watching television, while playing with toys and books, etc.

A child must first learn to recognize letters and numbers before learning to read words and calculate mathematical problems, and before moving on to read with understanding and perform more complicated computations with real-world application.

With the conventional emphasis on academic learning over imaginative play, children learn numbers, letters, word recognition, and counting at increasingly young ages. This does not, however, imply that a child will actually comprehend written language and mathematical concepts any earlier than a child who didn't learn the ABCs and 123s at as young of an age.

As children near preschool and kindergarten age, parents may begin to feel pressure to meet official early learning and developmental milestones. If we respond to this pressure by attempting to coerce our young children into accomplishing these goals, we risk passing on that pressure to our children.

Putting Pressure on Preschoolers
http://homeschooling.suite101.com

Much Too Early! by David Elkind
http://besthomeschooling.org

Initially, our children rebel against efforts to coerce them, but eventually they give in. Our urging squashes their natural curiosity and love of learning. When we appear discouraged by their progress, they likewise regard themselves as failures.

If we hold realistic learning goals for our children (i.e.,

acquisition of skills useful and desirable to them), we have nothing to worry about. If, on the other hand, our agendas tend toward prodigy or genius-level accomplishments in specialized interests, we may want to refocus on our children's personal interests and rethink our perception of success.

When I ask myself what I most want for my children, I readily answer: I want my children to live their own idea of success.

When worry, doubt, and fear of the future creep into our thinking, we can easily discern that our ambitions for our children have gone astray.

> Our children have all the time in the world to learn whatever they need to learn to accomplish whatever they want to accomplish.

Generations of unschooled children have proven that they learn naturally to read, write, and do mathematics according to their own schedules, in their own ways, for their own reasons. They learn these skills through a continuation of the same methods–playing, exploring, trying things out, and asking for guidance–used by very young children.

Some children pursue reading at five or six years old. Other children learn later. In any case, the child grows into a person who can read and do mathematics, perhaps even one who enjoys those activities.

My eldest daughter, Maia, views math as a fun, exciting tool. She jumps up and down and exclaims her satisfaction with each new challenging calculation. At her age, I perceived math as work that I had to do to get a good grade and thus to be a 'good, smart student.' The pressure and fear pained me.

Attempts to coerce earlier learning in a child who does not

yet have interest or ability will meet with the child's resistance and contribute to the development of a negative association with the subject, which may hinder future learning. Even when coercion does elicit early academic performance, the results may include unnecessary stress and harm to the child's self-image.

Children do learn 'the basics' over time through real-life experiences such as listening to stories read by their parents, cooking, gardening, solving puzzles, building, creating art, experimenting, etc. Some children choose to use conventional educational materials such as textbooks and workbooks. In any case, the progression of basic academic skills proceeds naturally according to children's needs, natural abilities, and interests.

Learning Styles

Conventional schooling does not support–or perhaps cannot support–a variety of learning styles. Conventional educational methods favor children who learn easily through listening to lectures and reading textbooks. For children who learn more easily in other ways, this prejudice can result in the perception of low general intelligence and misdiagnoses of learning disabilities.

In his book, *Frames of Mind: The Theory of Multiple Intelligences* (Basic Books, 1983), researcher and professor, Howard Gardner, proposed that we each possess at least seven basic intelligences with some types more prominent than others. In other words, rather than having one general level of intelligence, for better or worse, Mr. Gardner suggested that everyone has a unique ratio of intelligences (a.k.a. ways they perceive and learn). Gardner's seven intelligences include
- Linguistic,
- Logical-mathematical,
- Spatial,
- Bodily-kinesthetic,

- Musical,
- Interpersonal, and
- Intrapersonal.

Mr. Gardner has since added an eighth intelligence: Naturalistic intelligence, i.e, acute sensory awareness, memory. This intelligence compares with the 'highly sensitive' temperament, which some people mistake for attention-deficit, but which Richard Louv saw 'cured' in a natural setting (See Elaine Aron's *The Highly Sensitive Child* (Random House, 2002) and Richard Louv's *Last Child in the Woods* (Algonquin, 2005)).

Although I avoid limiting my perception of my children by applying labels to them, I do value Mr. Gardner's *multiple intelligences*, for increasing my awareness of the different ways people think and learn.

Unschooling parents maintain awareness of their children's strengths, abilities, and interests in order to open doors to activities that best meet each child's needs.

> The unschooling lifestyle gives children the freedom and flexibility to intuitively learn in the easiest and most enjoyable ways for them.

For example, rather than labeling Maia as a spacial/kinesthetic learner, or even as 'my little scientist' or 'my little artist,' I recognize that she learns best from visual presentations along with the freedom to move around a lot. She habitually paces while she performs math problems. In fact, she appears to *need* to move around while doing logical, cerebral types of activity, as if movement oils the gears in her brain for smooth functioning. ♡

My middle daughter, Ilana, quietly sings while she draws and prefers solitude for dance and imaginative play. She asks for privacy while she creates, and she shies away from structured group activities.

I acknowledge that my daughters express these

characteristics at the present time, and that they may change their habits and preferences at any time.

Linguistic. Children with strong linguistic ability learn easily from lectures, discussions, word games, storytelling, reading, writing, etc., given, of course, that they have interest in the subject and activity.

Logical-Mathematical. Children with strong logical ability learn easily from brain teasers, science experiments, number games, critical thinking, workbooks, etc.

Spatial. Children with strong spatial ability learn easily from visual presentations, art activities, metaphors, imagination games, etc.

Bodily-Kinesthetic. Children with strong kinesthetic ability learn easily from hands-on, physical activities, tactile experiences, drama, dance, relaxation exercises, etc.

Musical. Children with strong musical ability learn easily from songs, rhythms, etc. (Music involves mathematical concepts.)

Interpersonal. Children with strong interpersonal ability learn easily from group activities, peer tutoring, social gatherings, one-on-one conversations, etc.

Intrapersonal. Children with strong intrapersonal ability learn easily from individualized instruction, independent study, etc.

Naturalistic. Children with strong naturalist abilities show interest in acute sensory awareness, attention to subtle detail, and large stores of memory connections.

Action Styles

Just as we each have our own optimal style of learning, we also have personal approaches to getting started and proceeding through projects, problem solving, and other learning endeavors.

In an article entitled 'How to Be Wildly Successful,' published in *O Magazine* (January 2006), Martha Beck proposed four instinctive styles of action:

- Quick start (jump right in and figure it out, trial and error);
- Fact finder (seek information and instruction before beginning);
- Implementer (create models, physically manipulate the problem); and
- Follow-thru (create systems, methods, forms to follow).

Ms. Beck pointed out that mainly follow-thru types designed traditional schools, which may cause trouble for children who work differently.

Maia and I tend to jump right into the middle of a new project and learn as we go. We understand one another. "Come on, let's do it!" and we hit the ground running.

Ilana, conversely, takes a more cautious, watch-and-wait approach to new activities. She wants to read the instructions first, watch other people do the activity, and visualize herself doing it before taking her first step.

Despite having different ways of doing things, my daughters complement one another and work well together. ♡ For example, Maia typically gets the project started while Ilana observes, gathers more information, and prepares to see the project through to completion.

Learning Styles, Action Styles, and Unschooling
http://homeschooling.suite101.com

Homeschooling Styles

The spectrum of homeschooling approaches ranges from the most structured

Current estimates put the number of homeschoolers in the U.S. at 1.9 million.

school-at-home to the least structured radical unschooling lifestyle. Most homeschooling families fall somewhere in between and may change over time to suit the interests and needs of individual children, as well as of the family as an interrelated whole.

When people ask, I typically use the label *unschooling* to describe my family's homeschooling approach. By a limited definition, this informs people simply that we don't follow a curriculum. We may, however, *use* curricular materials for our own purposes. I rarely consult parent or teacher guides. Nonetheless, some interests inspire us to undertake structured projects while others inspire more creative endeavors.

School-at-Home. A majority of homeschoolers follow a structured curriculum program, or course of study, in imitation of traditional schooling with subjects, assignments, tests, grades, etc. The selected curriculum package, of which many varieties exist, typically includes lesson plans for parents and textbooks, assignments, and tests for the children.

The school-at-home approach to homeschooling may feel like an easier concept for parents to understand, because it resembles the experience many of us had in schools, and because Western culture promotes program following.

Unit Studies. Some curricular programs emphasize unit studies, which cover several subjects under one theme, i.e., a specific time period or location. The unit studies, or theme-based, approach may provide a more interesting presentation to children than a subject-by-subject approach, because integrating the subjects under a theme more closely imitates real life than, for example, extracting the math, science, literature, social studies, etc., from an event and teaching each subject separately.

Relaxed, Eclectic. Some homeschooling families practice a hybrid form between school-at-home and unschooling. For example, they may assign a curriculum for math, but allow the children to direct their own learning in other areas.

Unschooling. Unschoolers trust learning to occur spontaneously during the course of daily life. In this way, it may appear that an unschooler 'does nothing' much of the time.

At other times, with specific learning goals in mind, an unschooler may utilize educational materials along with any other tools or available resources, including instruction and direction (a.k.a. teaching), resulting in the appearance of an activity identical to that of a child doing curricular work. The unschooler, however, does the work by his or her own motivation.

An unschooler's desire to attend college, for example, manifests in focused, self-directed activity toward meeting specific entrance requirements.

My children enjoy using curricular materials. They like worksheets and educational DVDs and computer games. They take these educational materials and use them in their own ways. They do as little or as much paperwork as they desire. They watch as much of a video or play as much of a game as they feel the need for or inclination to do. When they need a break, they take one.

On the other hand, an unschooler may never use explicitly educational materials or engage in school-type activities.

Radical Unschooling. Whereas the term *unschooling* refers to learning, *radical unschooling* refers to living. Radical unschoolers, or *whole life learners*, apply unschooling ideals such as freedom and mutual respect to their whole lives. They don't perceive learning as separate from any other life activity, nor do they perceive parenting as separate from any other act of living.

The word *radical* means both 'root' and 'revolution.' Radical unschooling refers both to the root way of life, necessarily lacking arbitrary separation of the various life activities, and to revolution as a marked diversion from the conventional way of life in institutional culture.

Unschooling and radical unschooling concepts may seem more difficult for parents to understand, because they diverge far from the way most of us have lived. While we learn to live in a new way, we may go through a process, often called *deschooling* or *deprogramming*, during which we unlearn our previously held concepts about learning and raising children.

Many families find themselves at different points on the homeschooling spectrum at different times in their lives. Even within one family, multiple children may prefer varying levels of structure and guidance. Unschooling encourages parents to find the true, best fit for the family, honoring the needs of each family member.

Television, Internet, Video Games, & Junk Food

Television and other media such as Internet and video games, as well as junk food, often trigger mixed feelings. Popular unschooling philosophy holds that television and Internet bring the world to our children and that they will naturally self-regulate its usage if given the freedom to do so. Likewise for junk food.

I agree for the most part. Children do self-regulate *as best they can*. Nonetheless, I believe that my responsibility as parent to nurture my children includes creating and maintaining a safe home atmosphere and providing nourishing food.

I suspect that unschoolers, like many people in this culture, generally enjoy television programming, surfing the Web, playing video games, and eating tasty junk food. From this personal standpoint, we defend what we enjoy.

My husband plays video games and works as a professional game programmer. I knew that video games would play a part in my children's lives. What message would I send my children about their daddy by disallowing video games?

I watch my children with media and food. As long as they

enjoy and feel good with their activities and choices, I feel good, too. When I see that they do not feel good, such as by overconsuming or otherwise reacting negatively (my children have food allergies), I tell them what I see. We talk about it. I help them make the connection, so they can use that information for future choices.

I want my children to enjoy what they do, what they eat. I want them to feel happy and healthy. I listen to my intuition and let joy, not fear, guide me.

An Unschooling Course of Study on Australia

The following course of events illustrates how my children and I found ourselves surrounded by all things Australia. Neither did I plan to study Australia, nor had I previously had any but mild curiosity about the continent down under. Nonetheless, I began to see Australia at every turn.

- *Top Secret Adventures, Case #12455, Dilemma Down Under* (Highlights.com) sits on my desk.
- I just finished reading *Steve and Me* (Simon Spotlight Entertainment, 2008) by Terri Irwin, widow of "The Crocodile Hunter." My sister put that book in my hands, because Terri Irwin came from our hometown.
- While I read *Steve and Me*, I never had to consult the Australian dictionary, because I had already learned the common Strine words from the *Top Secret Adventures Guide to Australia*. I took frequent breaks from my reading to share anecdotes with my kids using words like *swag, billibong, and drongo*.
- After reading Terri Irwin's memoirs, I rented all the Crocodile Hunter documentaries (Netflix.com).
- The kids and I checked out a map of Australia and I pointed out the equator. We talked about how the earth turns in relation to the sun and how the seasons differ in the Northern and Southern Hemispheres. We

discovered that the middle of the Australian continent consists of a big desert and most folks live on the coasts.

- My daughters have watched an Australian television series about mermaids. The title of the show, H2O: Just Add Water (Jonathan M. Shiff, Film Finance, 2006), inspired an interest in chemical formulas.
- I downloaded two free trial games (BigFishGames.com), The Wild Thornberrys Australian Wildlife Rescue and Australia Zoo Quest.
- Now we really want to take a family vacation to Australia. My grandmother has visited Australia and has friends who live there. One of them called during our Christmas Eve party in the U.S. and their Christmas morning in Australia, prompting a discussion about the international date line.
- When I put *Steve and Me* back in my sister's hands, she gave me *Mutant Message Down Under* (Harper, 2004) by Marlo Morgan. I enjoyed it so much I located the next book, *Mutant Message From Forever*. Both books shared lots of aboriginal wisdom that I in turn shared with my children.

An on it goes…

From a series of unschooling courses of study
National Unschooling Examiner
http://www.examiner.com

Unschooling Philosophy

Beyond childhood learning, unschooling philosophy extends to parenting and all of life. It views learning as integral to living in the world. This chapter includes sections on
- Education,
- Definitions of unschooling,
- Daily life, and
- Unschooling advocates.

The unschooling frame of mind provides a way of seeing and living in the world. The unschooling lifestyle prompts us to maintain a level of awareness sufficient to honor and respect our children's and our own true needs.

When we support our children in taking responsibility for their own learning, *to own their learning*, we give them more than we could ever give them by directing their education. We give them trust, control in their lives, freedom, and boundless possibilities for personal success and enjoyment in life.

Get an Education?

As we may choose to use the words, *to help learn*, in place of, *to teach*, we may wish to better understand the common use of the word *education*.

When people speak of education, they typically say 'receive an education,' or 'get an education.' Both ways of wording it suggest a passive resignation to, or grudgingly active pursual of, this education thing–this package of standard knowledge.

Creating well-delineated definitions of the various terminology of learning and development can help us more clearly describe the unschooling approach to others, as well as to more fully comprehend it ourselves.

We all have unique interests and goals (passions, callings, dreams) for the present and the future. Our communities require a wide variety of skill sets. No common body of knowledge, no standard education, can meet the diverse needs of a community.

Nonetheless, a majority of children spend a significant amount of time and effort in educational programs, for which they may have little interest or use. Children and the adults in their lives could instead use this time nurturing unique talents and working toward fulfilling dreams.

Children, as well as adults, learn easily and joyfully when they choose to learn based on the interests and needs that make sense to them in a real-world way, rather than when they feel coerced or threatened into learning because someone else has appointed value to the information. When left to act according to their own motivations, children intuitively learn in the easiest way for them, and therefore build confidence in their ability to develop new skills, solve problems, and find wanted information.

We don't have to consciously think about the process of learning, because it happens naturally. When we encounter an obstacle to carrying out an activity, we learn what we need to know to meet the challenge.

People often ask my children, "What did you learn today?" but the question confuses my kids. They don't perceive their daily experiences in terms of academic subjects. They simply live each day as it comes, purposely going after topics of interest, spontaneously making discoveries, figuring out how to do new things, and honing other skills. They play with workbooks and art and building materials. They make discoveries while watching documentaries and have adventures while reading.

Unschoolers learn the 'subject areas,' the basics, in ways

that make sense through their individually-motivated daily experiences. For example, unschoolers may learn mathematical concepts through baking, building, computer programming, or by taking a math class or watching a video, depending on personal interests or learning styles.

A child with an interest in computer programming will, by necessity, follow that interest to advanced math skills. An interest in fashion design or architecture will lead to concepts in geometry. Baking may require conversions from one system of measurement to another and may even require algebra skills. These concepts and tools exist in the real world. Otherwise, why would we need them? Ask yourself, do you use square roots? If not, who does, and why? What for?

Unschoolers develop adept skills for finding ways to learn what they need to pursue their dreams. When unschooling parents don't already have the knowledge their children require, they help the children find it through a multitude of resources (i.e., apprenticeship, library card, yellow pages, Internet, experts, tutors, masters, practitioners, etc.)

Definitions of Unschooling

1. Unschooling: Learning by doing, wondering, and figuring things out.

Natural, self-directed, interest-driven learning follows the learner's own agenda. The learner proceeds naturally, interest by interest, along a lifelong journey in pursuit of knowledge and experiences that each serve a meaningful purpose in the learner's life.

My daughter, Maia, feels especially drawn to marine life, ancient life, and the water world. She wants to study, help protect, train, and otherwise work with marine mammals, as well as work in the paleontology field.

We make frequent visits to local shores, as well as the local aquarium where Maia plans to apply for the teen volunteer apprenticeship program. In the meantime, she plans to attend aquarium classes and camps for younger children, as well as to seek out other opportunities toward her goal. When we travel, we visit shores and aquariums.

Maia's interests in marine life and ancient life have led her to watch documentaries about dinosaurs, paleontologists, biologists, divers, film-makers, aquariums around the world, whales and dolphins, ancient ocean life, the plight of coral reefs, etc. She studies marine life and ancient life in encyclopedias and collects figures of marine mammals, amphibians, dinosaurs, and dragons.

Her interests, which began with marine mammals and dinosaurs, has grown to include habitats, plant life, fish and sharks, shore birds, animal training, diving, tide pools, islands, weather, magnetism, and on and on.

Along this course, my daughters have watched several television series featuring ancient mammals and reptiles, as

Pop Bottle Science
http://workman.com

well as a series about mermaids in which the antagonist marine biologist's scientific curiosity has caused her to lose sight of the natural rights of ocean life. Even the title of the show, *H2O: Just Add Water* (Jonathan M. Shiff, Film Finance, 2006), inspired my daughters' interest in chemical formulas, which led to numerous pop-bottle science experiments.

These interests have introduced my daughters to many so-called academic areas (biology, ecology, chemistry, earth and weather sciences, mathematics, environmental conservation, etc.) in an integrated, real-world way. Their pursuit of information involves activities that they choose and engage in freely, such as reading books, watching videos, taking trips to zoos, museums, and beaches, talking with professionals, and attending classes and camps. In this way, their way, they learn much more readily and rapidly, fueled by their own curiosity and excitement for discovery.

2. Unschooling: Learning without schooling.

Unschooling describes learning through life's experiences. Learning does not require schooling or teaching. The act of teaching includes an offer of information, at best, and pressure or threat to learn, at worst.

Rather than teaching in this negative sense, unschooling parents help children learn by including them in daily activities, remaining available, answering questions, and assisting children in finding answers and learning new skills.

In addition, unschooling parents set the scene for learning by providing children with a rich environment and access to resources.

Unschooling in Daily Life

Family dynamics vary from one unschooling family to another. One or both parents may work in the home. The children may span from very young, adolescent, or range in age.

Some families follow daily routines that include mealtimes, outside errands, or the running of a family business. Children may spend some time alone reading, playing, creating, or experimenting, and they may spend some time with siblings, parents, tutors, or caregivers.

Children may run errands or participate in work with their parents, or attend music classes, scout groups, homeschool clubs, or volunteer jobs outside their homes.

Some days children may appear to learn productively while other days they appear to do nothing at all.

> We all need periods of activity and rest.

Appearances can deceive. A lot of processing happens during rest days. We need inwardly-focused days and rest days. Likewise, days full of play and imagination can provide a child with the opportunity to explore new ideas and develop new interests that will lead to more focused learning in the future. Children's interests and the ways they pursue those interests change over time. An active, playful young child may turn serious and focused as an older child. A formerly independent child may suddenly require more assistance. The unschooling parent responds by maintaining trust, sensitivity, and the willingness provide support and guidance in whatever form the child needs.

For my family, each day of the week looks somewhat different. I work at home and have a flexible schedule. My youngest daughter presently breastfeeds and my older two daughters have reached different stages of dependence.

My older two daughters spend portions of the day alone and together. They use their computers to surf the

> LEGO Education
> http://legoeducation.us

Web, play video games, and use art software. They play make-believe games with dolls and animal figures. They build simple machines and other constructions with LEGO blocks or with straws and shaving cream or other puzzles and kits. They draw, paint, and cut and paste to make all sorts of artworks. They watch videos of all kinds. They read books. They invent things when they see a need or simply when they feel adventurous.

Together we do science experiments, play in the garden, paint, do arts and crafts projects, read magazines, do house chores, and whatever else. We regularly set out a big pile of books and magazines on a current interest with which we sit and read as we desire throughout the day.

My baby often observes these activities from a soft baby carrier worn on my back. The practice of babywearing

> The Baby Wearer
> http://thebabywearer.com

allows me to get many of my responsibilities accomplished, as well as provides my baby with an elevated view and loft from which to participate in projects.

My family does not typically follow a schedule, but over time we have created comfortable routines. We wake at around the same time each morning and wind down and get in bed at around the same time each night. Typically, I and my husband alternate reading a story to our children while they fall asleep. They and I share one series of stories while he and they share another.

I prepare a couple of meals during the day at roughly the same time, otherwise we nibble from a snack tray that I keep stocked with a changing array of finger foods and dips (similar in concept to our book buffet offer of new experiences and information.)

We run a typical set of errands most days–post office, grocery store, perhaps the drug store or hardware store. My children go everywhere with me and learn to do the things I do. They sum up purchases and pay at the grocery store. My middle daughter, Ilana, loves to push the cart and unload the groceries at check out. They mail and pick up packages at the post office. Clerks around town know them by name.

We have a few scheduled appointments for which we have to arrive on time. We pick up a box of vegetables from a local farm each week during the harvest season. We attend a play date at the park once a week. My children often attend regular activities with our local homeschool group or take classes at the local dance studio, art center, martial arts center, or other community class offering that catch their interests.

We adapt our routine to the seasons, to my children's interests, and to my work schedule. We approach our lifestyle as a creative project.

A Note on Chores

When I mention household chores, I don't mean chores assigned to the children. I refer to maintenance of the home that any one of us may do.

In my family, we have never assigned chores, yet each of the children spontaneously offers to do them when they see the need. We live in partnership and speak of the home and maintenance as all of ours.

Sometimes I clean their bedroom, because I prefer a tidy home or want to improve the emotional atmosphere. Other times they clean it, because they need floor space or want to improve the feel of their room.

My eldest daughter, Maia, refers to herself as "junior mother," and actively seeks out ways to help me care for her younger siblings. Ilana *really* enjoys doing dishes. My daughters want to help and learn the skills required to keep house and care for children.

I expect my children to help around the house just as I expect them to learn everything they need to learn to function well in life. I expect it, because it happens naturally when people live together in partnership.

I have heard people suggest that they would feel resentful if they did most of the cleaning. I can relate to that, because my thoughts sometimes drift into a negative outlook, especially if I feel overtired or stressed.

I don't have to feel this way, however. I can choose to feel good about making a peaceful or beautiful home atmosphere for my family. Or I can choose not to clean when my energy feels low.

I own that I prefer a tidy house and that I feel better in one. Therefore, I acknowledge that I clean for myself.

Unschooling Advocates

I have read extensively about education, especially early childhood education and unschooling. Those authors each contributed something new to my personal philosophy.

> "Adam was the only man who, when he said a good thing, knew that nobody had said it before him."–Mark Twain (Samuel Clemens) *Notebook*, 1867.

Although I have worked in several child care institutions where the children called me teacher, I have never worked as a certified school teacher. My children have never attended school. My primary knowledge of schooling comes from many years of my own childhood experiences in public school.

Several of the following prominent advocates of unschooling have taught in schools and have extensive experience working in the education system. I have chosen to specifically note teachers-turned-advocates in this section. You can find additional advocates in the Bookshelf chapter at the end of the book.

John Caldwell Holt coined the term *unschooling*. He taught in private schools for many years before writing his

> John Holt & GWS
> *http://www.holtgws.com*

first books *How Children Fail* (Da Capo Press, 1964) and *How Children Learn* (Da Capo Press, 1967). He advocated for school reform by speaking and writing books that explored education theory and practice, children's rights, alternative schools, and many other social issues related to schooling.

Holt's focus eventually changed from school reform to alternatives to schooling. In 1977, he started the first homeschooling magazine, *Growing Without Schooling*. His last two books, the only two specifically about homeschooling, include *Teach Your Own* (Da Capo Press, 1981) and *Learning All The Time* (Da Capo Press, 1989).

Patrick Farenga authored *The Beginner's Guide To*

Homeschooling (Holt Associates, 2000), revised and republished John Holt's *Teach Your Own* (Perseus Books, 2003), and continues John Holt's advocacy work. He currently holds the position of President of Holt Associates, Inc., and published *Growing Without Schooling* magazine from 1985, after John Holt's death, until it stopped publishing in November 2001.

Susannah Sheffer authored *A Life Worth Living: Selected Letters of John Holt* (Ohio State University Press, 1991), *Writing Because We Love To* (Boynton/Cook, 1992), and *A Sense of Self* (Boynton/Cook, 1997). She edited *Growing Without Schooling* magazine.

Matt Hern, Ph.D., authored *Deschooling Our Lives* (New Society, 1998), *Field Day* (New Star Books, 2003), and *Everywhere All the Time* (AK Press, 2008). He ran an alternative school for young children and worked with a large public free school and an alternative-to-school teen center.

Sandra Dodd authored *Sandra Dodd's Big Book of Unschooling* (Lulu, 2009). She taught junior high school before

> Sandra Dodd
> *http://sandradodd.com*

becoming an advocate of unschooling. From 1998, she edited the *Home Education Magazine* online newsletter and hosted a weekly unschooling chat. Her website provides articles on many aspects of a radical unschooling lifestyle.

Grace Llewellyn authored *The Teenage Liberation Handbook* (Lowry House, 1998) and *Guerilla Learning* (Wiley,

> Not Back to School Camp
> *http://nbtsc.org*

2001). She taught middle school English. She leads an annual Not Back to School Camp in Oregon and Vermont.

John Taylor Gatto authored *Dumbing Us Down* (New Society Publishers, 1992) and *Weapons of Mass Instruction* (New Society Publishers, 2008). He earned New York's Teacher of the Year award.

John Taylor Gatto
http://johntaylorgatto.com

Deschooling

The noncoercive nature of an unschooling lifestyle may cause some parents, especially those who attended conventional school themselves, to experience some transient feelings of insecurity and loss of control, particularly when faced with concern or criticism from friends and relatives. This chapter includes sections on

- Doubts and fears,
- Deprogramming,
- School life,
- Whole life,
- Conversations with relatives, and
- Legal learning requirements.

Even as we settle more naturally into the world of unschooling, we may still worry about how our children's self-motivated, growing body of knowledge and experience compares to that of average conventionally schooled children. Without grades or test scores, we don't have a measurement to easily satisfy fearful friends and relatives.

Since most of us attended conventional schools, and didn't choose our own learning experiences, we sometimes have difficulty letting go of the pattern of control and expectations to which we feel accustomed. Before coming to a place of trust, we may go through a process called deschooling in which we overwrite years of cultural programming.

Doubts and Fears

Perhaps the most difficult aspect of unschooling requires giving up the illusion of control and instead trusting and allowing our children to learn what they personally need to learn.

For many parents, we believe it when we see it, and our unschooled children don't disappoint us in this. We may not measure our children's learning by units, but we see that they continue learning. My daughters enthusiastically share with me whatever new topic they have discovered. ♡ I witness that they continue progressing and developing at a rapid rate, just as they did during babyhood.

Nonetheless, some parents fear that their unschooled children will not learn all the subject areas mandated by standard school curricula, and therefore will not build an adequate foundation for college or work life.

Conventional schooling provides a standardized education in the form of a curriculum divided by age and further by subject categories. Conventionally schooled children digest topics according to the same schedule.

Unschoolers, conversely, each make their own individual learning schedules that may vary widely from those used in schools. However, unschoolers do demonstrate that they learn traditional academic subjects through the pursuit of personally-motivated activities.

For example, my daughters have covered our state's mandated general academic learning standards for social studies, science, language arts, health and safety, and mathematics, through activities of their own choosing. I know that they have learned these things in the same way that I know they can read, compose songs and poems, skip rope, do hip hop dance moves, recognize scores of dinosaurs, and identify plants and animals in our garden. We live together. We talk. We do things together.

Maia composed her first poem during a walk to the grocery store. On a chilly day toward the end of autumn she began repeating lines in rhythm with her steps, "No more colory leaves. Only bare trees. No more colory leaves. Only bare trees." By the time we finished shopping and had nearly arrived home again, she completed her poem.

> No more colory leaves
> Only bare trees
> Winter is coming soon
> Better hide your little leaves
> 'Cause Winter is coming soon.
> –Maia McGrath, age 6

Over the course of eighteen years, I not only trust, but confidently expect that my children will have acquired at least the same basic body of knowledge as any other person in this culture. According to my state's official learning goals, an educated child should be able to

- Read, write, and communicate effectively;
- Think creatively and logically to solve problems; and
- Set and work toward goals.

From this broader perspective, I see without a doubt that my children continue progressing beautifully. ♡

Deprogramming

Years of institutional programming cause many parents to automatically, habitually view learning according to officially established subject categories, such as social studies, science, language arts, health, and mathematics.

Unschoolers approach these topics from a variety of perspectives. For example, my daughters study animals from the perspectives of a biologist, naturalist, artist, farmer, zoologist, veterinarian, trainer, breeder, welfare worker, conservationist, etc. We purposefully look for people who live my children's interests. In this way, categories overlap, blend, and move toward indistinguishability.

Subject divisions that apply in the school setting don't

necessarily apply in life. Language arts, social studies, science, arts, math, physical education, etc., interrelate and integrate in the real world. Music uses math and science occurred in history.

Can you define science? Biology, botany, chemistry, physics. In reality, these topics and tools of study both diverge and interrelate, depending on the circumstances of use.

I received a 'C' grade in my first semester of high school biology. After that unsatisfactory grade (failure), I didn't hold out much hope that I would do better in chemistry or physics, because I linked them as sciences in my mind.

Likewise, I received a 'C' grade in the last math class I ever took To me, a 'C' proved that I could not do well in math. Fortunately, unschooled children rarely, if ever, think in this way.

Regardless of the receipt of a standardized education designed to create productive members of society, each person has his or her own strengths, talents, and interests. The world needs community members with a wide variety of skills and passions.

> Unschoolers design their own lives and find their place by doing what they love and following what calls to them.

When Maia suggested that she wanted to dance or play rock music as an occupation, I said, "That sounds great!" whereas a more conventional response would discourage her from an impractical dream.

When I told a favorite teacher that I wanted to paint or write novels, or even both!, he responded with a dream-extinguishing word: "impractical." I heard "stupid," "pointless," and "You don't have the talent." It took me years and years, well into adulthood, before I resumed pursuing those dreams.

For as long as my daughter wants to purse the dream of playing in a rock band or discovering proof of living plesiosaurs, I will fully support and help her in every way. ♡

School Life

Unschoolers experience learning as the satisfaction of natural curiosity and the acquisition of useful tools.

Those of us who did most of our focused learning in a school setting experienced learning in a markedly different way, i.e, not for the sake of learning something in particular, but as a discipline required to place a grade on a transcript, perhaps to please parents, or to earn entrance to a college and ultimately to this culture's idea of success: a high-paying, powerful job position with fame as a bonus.

The school learning process directs children toward a vaguely defined future reward. The learning done in school may not even result in real learning, but rather temporary memorization or on-the-spot deduction sufficient to pass a test. School children learn to persevere through years of unpleasant activities in hope of eventual freedom and rest, along with a job.

Without pressure toward the contrary, our unschooling children live their lives from moment to moment. They seek joy in everything they do, otherwise they would sense no purpose for doing a thing.

My childhood life revolved around school. I remember lamenting, especially in the wintertime, that I spent nearly all of the daylight hours indoors in an artificially-lit classroom in a stone building with no windows. When I finally got home each evening, I spent hours on homework, often until bedtime. Even clarinet practice, which I had enjoyed when I began years earlier, felt like a drill.

Under other circumstances, I may have enjoyed learning about the topics that the teachers covered in school. Instead, I felt the pressure of deadlines and grading on a curve, which pitted me and my classmates against one another, and threatened my grade point average and my future college opportunities. My classmates and I also competed for positions on the limited enrollment honor role.

For two years, I managed to stay in the high school honors program with a GPA in the top three percent at my school, yet my life felt like an endless grind. I disciplined myself to keep up the work with my eyes on the promised prize–graduation, college, high-paying career, and finally, peace and happiness.

The closer I got to finishing high school, the more anxious I felt about my future college and career. I secretly most wanted, from my earliest childhood ambitions, to have children and care for them. However, no one talked about motherhood as an ambition, so I pushed my true desire down and kept to the prescribed, vaguely aimed educational path that had dominated most of my life.

At age 16, I dropped out of high school and easily passed the General Educational Development (GED) high school equivalency test offered by the local community college. My three younger siblings shortly followed suit.

Leaving high school two years early marked my first step in taking responsibility and realizing the possibilities for my own future. I now see my escape from high school as the liberation of my heart and mind.

In the years that followed, I rediscovered joy in learning. I proceeded to learn, through a combination of ways, whatever I wanted to learn. I took art and writing classes and workshops. I read books. I did these things, no longer for the purpose of getting a job and proving myself to others, but for my own self enrichment.

Whole Life

Some homeschooling parents attempt to separate learning activities from the rest of family life. Likewise, some conventional parents attempt to separate their child-rearing responsibilities from the rest of life. A homeschooling family may create separation by setting aside blocks of time for compulsory learning, perhaps in designated learning areas.

Unschooling families, on the other hand, live together as partners in whole, integrated lives, free of illusory divisions. We know that we cannot live without learning and need not designate time especially for learning.

Unschooling children rarely perceive a distinct separation between things they do and things they learn. Learning simply happens, often without the conscious knowledge of the learner.

Unschooling children feel comfortable in their world. Their parents act as real-world role models and welcome the children to participate in 'adult' activities. Unschooling children develop a level of confidence and self-awareness we rarely see in schooled people.

Unschoolers have the time and freedom to get to know themselves and the other people in their lives. They tend to more comfortably interact with adults than do schooled children who must view their elders as superiors. Unschoolers have the freedom to value and respect the expertise of adults who can provide learning experiences and opportunities. My children spontaneously express gratitude to me, their dad, and their various community teachers.

Unschooling children who formerly attended school may need some time to deschool to disappear the arbitrary divisions in their lives. However, due to the natural flexibility and adaptability of children, they may have an easier process than would a fully-schooled adult.

Much of life feels relatively new to children. With new experiences, they continually form and change big ideas. They continue exploring and discovering their thoughts and feelings about how they live or may want to live differently.

When former school children begin unschooling, all of a sudden their lives feel lighter and freer. At first they may resist activities which they interpret as educational (at least those in which they consciously recognize the teaching), but in time they lose the defensive response, relax, and regain their natural curiosity and simple joy in learning and doing new things. You can do it, too.

Conversations with Relatives

It often amazes me how much interest and concern random people express for unschooling children. Concerned friends and relatives with no personal experience of homeschooling imagine that the children will have limited learning opportunities, will lack social experiences, or will have trouble getting into college or adapting to work life.

You can attempt to dispel these fears by sharing the wide variety of learning opportunities available to homeschoolers, the real-life social and learning experiences available through your community, and the fact that generations of homeschoolers attend and succeed in colleges and careers.

However, if your answers don't convince others, try not to worry about it. Just as you cannot teach unreceptive children, you cannot reach unreceptive adults.

You need not defend your choices or prove yourself or your children. You need not engage in arguments simply because someone challenges your choices. If you like, you can return challenging questions with questions of your own. Ask why.

Fears arise from things we don't understand, things we have little or no knowledge of or experience with. The majority of people in Western culture attended school and many believe children need school to grow into competent adults. They haven't imagined any other way.

Legal Learning Requirements

Depending on where you live, your local school district or government agency may dictate learning requirements for your children. Governments typically accomplish the regulation of homeschoolers through documentation requirements or annual testing or assessment. Local homeschool associations or groups often provide the best source of practical interpretations and requirements of homeschool law.

Some localities have requirements for homeschooling parents, such as

- Completing a parent qualifying course;
- Having previously completed a minimum number of college credits;
- Meeting periodically with a certified teacher; or
- Receiving approval from the local government.

Academic standards or learning requirements don't typically dictate the learning method or style, but simply provide performance expectations for each grade level.

Under my local government's 'home-based education' laws, my family has had no trouble satisfying legal learning requirements (a.k.a. academic standards, grade level expectations, or performance expectations).

Documentation. With a little creativity, you can translate your unschooling children's learning activities into the institutional language and format that school and government officials understand and prefer. For example, hanging out at the beach at low tide translates as a 'field trip,' perhaps with 'hands-on activities' and lessons in earth science, magnetism, chemistry, biology, etc.

Sometimes, as they gain more knowledge of institutional expectations, unschooling children fall prey to worry over how their academic achievements measure up with schooled peers. They may feel pressure from peers or relatives. If this happens, your children can look over a list of general academic standards to make their own assessment.

World Book encyclopedia prepares a Typical Course of Study, generalized across North America, for preschool through 12th grade levels. You and your children can use this as a checklist or as a source of ideas for topics and skills to pursue. Oftentimes, consultation of such a list puts unschoolers at ease. What looks like a long list of requirements includes a lot of repetition and common sense.

Unschoolers exist all over the world. Find them, join together in community, and help one another navigate homeschool laws, as well as to challenge legislation and protect freedoms when necessary.

World Book
http://worldbook.com/wb/Students?curriculum

Printable Checklists
http://homeschool-curricula.suite101.com/
article.cfm/homeschool_curriculum
_standards_checklists

Learning Environment

Unschooling parents support their children by providing a rich learning atmosphere full of possibilities and free of pressure. This chapter includes sections on
- Supplies,
- Enriching,
- Family life, and
- Daily activities.

Although unschooling families spend varying amounts of time at home, home typically serves as home base. My children do many of their learning activities at home and launch most of their adventures from home. Creating the space we live in involves a lot of fun activity for the whole family.

You will discover endless possibilities in everyday objects and in the multitude of people in your life. Access to interesting people and interesting things adds to a rich learning atmosphere.

Each family works differently and each child has different needs and interests, so the space each family creates has a unique look and feel. You may begin to see your home and the homes of others through newly curious eyes.

Enriching your home need not cost a lot. Homeschooling families live within many different budgets and use a variety of ways to explore their interests with little financial investment. Think library, skills sharing, book swaps, etc.

Where a family lives, their proximity to community resources, and their finances influence whether they choose to fill their homes with an abundance of educational materials or whether to rely more on outside resources.

Supplies and Other Stuff

Anything goes. Household objects, craft supplies, books, texts, encyclopedias, workbooks, videos, computers, Internet, video games, natural objects, garden tools, kitchen supplies, etc.–children can use all these things in the pursuit of information and experience. You can purchase educational materials and other things, borrow books and DVDs from the local library, purchase used supplies from yard sales and thrift shops, and share materials among a group of homeschooling families.

Local homeschool groups often put together supply swaps and shares. Other sources of community giving, swaps, shares, and sales of used goods include the following.

- Freecycle, *http://freecycle.org*
- Paperback Swap, *http://paperbackswap.com*
- Edify at Home, *http://edifyathome.com*
- eBay, *http://ebay.com*

Homeschooling need not tax the family's budget. In fact, according to recent research comparing homeschoolers' test results to those of public school students, homeschooling families spend dramatically less money per year ($600 average) per student than public schools ($10,000 average) with significantly better results [Dr. Brian Ray. Progress Report 2009: Homeschool Academic Achievement and Demographics. National Home Education Research Institute (NHERI), 2009].

Books. Books provide easily accessible information. My children's many favorite publishers include Usborne, Scholastic, Random House, and Klutz.

> *Wright on Time*, an adventure series by Lisa Cottrell-Bentley, features an unschooling family.
> *http://wrightontimebooks.com*

Rather than the more conventional television room, the

front room of our house serves as the family library. Bookshelves line the walls and share space with one sofa, one comfy chair, one narrow table against the wall, and books everywhere.

My daughters enjoy creating book collections on their favorite subjects (dinosaurs, horses and ponies, marine life, mythology, etc.). We have had many, many books gifted to us from other families whose children outgrew them. We enjoy loading up the wagon with books that we have outgrown and exchanging them at the local used bookstore. I often search eBay for inexpensive collections of books, such as *The Magic School Bus* series, which my children especially love.

Arts and Crafts. College bookstores, art supply stores, and craft stores typically provide quality arts and crafts supplies. My children also enjoy the benefit of an abundance of art supplies from my college days during the time when I worked toward a fine arts degree.

If your children's artistic style tends toward quantity, a roll of drawing paper to fit a dispenser or easel provides an inexpensive way to keep them supplied with ready paper. Chalk, pencils, watercolor paints, sponges, crayons, marker pens, etc., cost relatively little. Budget Art Kids provides all non-toxic art and craft materials with kids in mind.

Budget Art Kids
http://budgetartkids.com

Discount Dance Supply
http://discountdance.com

Music. Make music. Play music. Listen to music. Try not to learn music. Let practice go the way of school work. Give your children instruments and they will play.

My daughters have made surprisingly beautiful and creative music with guitars, keyboards, harmonicas, hand drums, rattles, tambourines, their voices, their bodies, etc., since very young ages.

I watch a video of Ilana at age three playing her guitar and singing a song of her own composition, and I find myself awestruck at how naturally melodic, rhythmic, and beautiful her music sounds. ♡

I found a chart of 'small-hand chords' and placed it on the wall near the guitars. My children have had no formal musical instruction, yet Maia at age six read the guitar tablature and played the chords for me.

In a similar manner, Maia declared that she would play Mary Had A Little Lamb on her recorder. She did so despite never having received any instruction in note reading or recorder playing. She had used an available book and figured out what she wanted to do. Only after establishing her ability for herself did she show receptivity to further instruction from me.

Drums make intuitive first instruments. My youngest daughter, Kalea, has played drums since about four months of age. When I saw that she enjoyed clapping and slapping her body to make music, I handed her a drum. She repeats rhythms that we listen to on CD and she makes up her own. We have since attended Musikgarten classes together.

Remo Percussion makes professional-quality children's drums. My family has several Remo drums, as well as

> Remo Percussion
> *http://www.remo.com*

several lovely-sounding department store toy drums.

My daughters have their dad's ancient cassette player in their bedroom along with my teenage music collection, as well as cassettes collected from other relatives.

Each summer, we attend our town's free concerts in the park, enjoy an assortment of local music, and get to dance in the park with our neighbors.

Educational Materials. My children typically enjoy workbooks, puzzle books, encyclopedias, science kits, and other overtly educational product. Homeschool curriculum fairs provide one source of curriculum packages, books, arts and crafts supplies, classes and programs, etc. We look forward to the LEGO and Usborne booths.

My children especially love informational book series' such as

- *The Magic School Bus* (Scholastic), science;
- *Magic Tree House* (Random House), history and geography; and
- *Max Axiom* (Capstone Press), graphic science.
- *Chester Comix* (Bentley Boyd), graphic history.

Homeschoolers can take advantage of price reductions on many things during the school year as well as of end-of-school-year clearance sales and homeschool group discounts.

Homeschool Buyers Co-op
https://homeschoolbuyersco-op.org/?source=21877
(The source number gives my family extra points.)

Enriching

Unschooling advocate, Sandra Dodd, promotes a practice which she calls *strewing*. This refers to the placement of interesting things around the house where children may discover them. My daughters inspired me to call our version of the practice *sprinkling*, after the image of a fairy with a magic wand sprinkling our home with gifts and surprises. ♡ I also refer to it as enriching the home.

Take a sprinkling of fairy dust,
An angel's single feather,
Also a dash of love and care,
Then mix them both together.
Add a sentiment or two,
A thoughtful wish or line,
A touch of stardust, a sunshine ray...
It's a recipe for a baby girl truly fine.
–Author unknown.

Enriching your home may involve rolling a fresh area of paper over an easel, setting out colored pencils, placing books or magazines on a low shelf, or setting out workbooks, games, videos, sports equipment, musical instruments, etc.

I sprinkle my children's snack tray with new foods. When we get a new vegetable in our weekly farm share box, I open our produce guide to the corresponding page and set it on the table. When I spot something interesting in the grocery store produce department, such as fractal broccoli or orange cauliflower, I usually get it. Then I may mention fractals and the family of cruciferous vegetables to see if the kids want to hear more.

Many parents already rotate toys in and out of areas where their children play. This practice can make old toys feel fresh and interesting again and may cut down on the number of new toys you buy. When I notice that my children have not played with something in a while, I rotate it into storage and exchange it for something they have not seen in a while. Several areas in our house get so crowded that my children gratefully pack things away to reduce clutter.

Open spaces refresh us and open us up to creativity. An

empty table and neatly ordered papers, pens, pencils, etc., beg us to use them.

We borrow interesting things from the library and from friends and family and make inexpensive purchases from used and discount sources. Items need not have specific educational purpose to spark interest. For example, river rocks could lead to many exciting adventures (geology, geography, energy, fossils, mining, archeology, etc.) My daughters love the free rock and gem shows, as well as our own rock hunting outings.

Old toys kept by grandparents could lead to projects in genealogy, history, toy-making, technology, etc. When my mother-in-law gifted us with an old set of baby silverware that required polishing, Maia embarked on a study of metals. My husband gleefully told her everything he knew about the subject from basic elements to medieval weapons and tool smithing.

Ilana often surprises me by expressing interest in possessions of mine which I would never have guessed would appeal to her. At two years old, she asked me to hand her a deck of tarot cards which I kept out of her reach, unintentionally. After looking through them, she asked for the accompanying book. She then proceeded to match each card to its description page in the book. We then talked about archetypal images, which she had familiarity with through folk tales.

Sandra Dodd extends strewing to taking her children places where they can discover things they may not have otherwise discovered. These places include garage sales, old stores, new stores, flea markets, vacant lots, natural areas, etc.

My daughters and I recently wound our way through a cluttered, but fascinating antique store. It reminded me of my great grandmother's apartment, so we talked about her and her nicknacks, as well as about the 50s, porcelain dolls, vinyl records, accordions, etc. ♡

My daughters felt drawn to some antique fishing lures and

we talked about those, too. That led to a fishing trip, casting practice in the backyard pool, study of a children's fishing guide, a series of children's books on fly fishing, talk of their Papa who loved fishing, and ongoing interest in all things related to fishing.

My daughters express equal excitement about a trip to a new department store as to the zoo or other recreational destination. I remember the sense of exploration and discovery that 'window shopping' provided me and my siblings during our childhoods. I suspect my daughters experience similar feelings even when we go for a walk, taking a different route than the time before.

When my daughters dawdle when I would rather rush to and fro on a routine errand, I remind myself that the world feels new and interesting to children. They remind me of this by pointing out flower buds and caterpillars that I may have otherwise rushed past.

Family Life

During their first couple of years, I watched the way Ilana and Kalea watched their older sister with awe and imitated many of the things she did. She, herself, it seemed, provided the most interesting thing to them for some time, perhaps because she represented their own near-future potential.

People to learn from, perhaps, serve a more important purpose than materials. The people at home and nearby serve as children's first models. When children see us reading, writing, using money, etc., they show interest in doing so also, or at least in understanding why we do these things.

Children grow into adults, so they seek to learn about adults. They watch us and other adults in their lives. We can provide them with opportunities to take part in our regular activities, such as house chores, errands, hobbies, etc. As much as I sometimes just want to get a daily chore done, I slow down when Kalea wants to pull laundry from the dryer or splash in the dish water. ♡ Likewise, Maia and Ilana regularly want to try out cooking, child care, and most of my routine activities. Both of them create their own books and spend some time at the computer each day, too.

With me typing away at the computer and my husband creating and playing video games, it comes as no surprise that our children feel drawn to computers. They each have their own and have used them independently from about age three. Maia's desire to navigate the computer menus inspired her to learn to read.

Parents, as well as siblings and others in an unschooling home, typically spend some time participating in games and projects, and other times simply remaining available to answer questions or help in the pursuit of a child's interests or the solving of problems. Younger children typically ask more questions because they don't yet know how to find answers for themselves. When you don't know the answer to a question, show your children how to go about finding it and soon they will find more and more of their own answers.

For example, Maia used to come to me with every word she didn't know. I showed her how to use the dictionary and she started excitedly coming to me to share definitions. She discovered encyclopedias next, followed by other reference books (thesauruses, atlases, etc.) I see grammar guides in her future.

My daughters have their dad's childhood collection of *Childcraft Annual* children's encyclopedias (World Book, c.1970-1980), which they cherish because of that history. ♡ They also have a couple of children's books that belonged to both me and their dad as young children.

Children will, at different times, prefer solo or group activities, structured or unstructured activities, focused learning or imaginative play. Sometimes your children may prefer to follow their own interests, other times they will express curiosity about yours. Take your cues from them. You can certainly offer information or suggest an activity, but if they resist, let it go until another time.

I focus on my role as parent. My children want me to do what I do so they can learn from me. When they have interests which I know little or nothing about, I help them find people who do know about those interests, not necessarily teachers, but real people who do that work or that hobby or whatever because they love to do it.

Friends, relatives, and homeschooling support group members can pool their expertise and offer it to all the children in the family or group. Everyone has an area of expertise, from computer programming to auto repair, carpentry, or domestic work.

My daughters have a great-grandmother who makes custom clothing patterns, another grandmother who makes quilts and owned a quilting store, a dad who programs video games, and a mom who does mother work, which they aspire to do, and who has a passion for naturalist skills, folk music, and storytelling.

Our neighbors include a musician and a boat builder. Our town has great dance instructors, art teachers, and a children's librarian who always remembers my daughters' names and asks them how they are doing, as do the cashiers at the grocery store and the clerks at the post office. We have taken tours of the local police department, post office, and pet store.

During my early childhood, my grandmother showed me how to sew, follow a recipe, tend and harvest the garden, and can food. Our local senior center offers classes to families which demonstrate those skills, too. Opportunities abound.

Daily Activities

Order in an unschooling household typically works through routines rather than schedules. At my house, we have familiar routines which involve my children doing some activities on their own, and some time interacting with me, one another, or people outside the home.

A day in the life of Ilana, for example, may include some time playing by herself, drawing, dancing, singing, doing puzzles, playing with dolls, or some other make-believe game. Later, she may choose to join me in preparing a meal or doing household chores, or she may ask to watch a video or listen to music. She often asks me to turn on her computer, play games with her, or read to her. ♡

Maia, likewise, spends some time by herself doing puzzle books and online lessons, playing video games, watching videos, or some other project. Later, she may spend time in the garden or at the neighbor's house.

My daughters each attend classes in the community and regular activities with our local homeschool groups. We belong to the state association, a local homeschool group, a local unschooling group. We also started a play club for our town.

My children tend to focus on particular interests in cycles. For example, Maia has presently chosen to take a sabbatical break from art classes for a session. In the mean time, she has shifted her creative attention to hand crafts, fashion design, and dance. She took a similar break from ballet, during which she danced on her own at home, before returning for further formal instruction.

On most days, my children use various forms of technology, including online videos (Netflix, Totlol), several online subscriptions (JumpStart, BrainPOP, Discovery Streaming), and a variety of websites and computer software.

Some unschooling parents readily embrace the possibilities provided by television, videos, DVDs, computer games, Internet, audiotapes, etc, while others express fears. Arguments for limiting or excluding 'screen time' activities, in general:

- TV and video games harm, or at least don't benefit children;
- TV and video games eat up time which children could

spend doing more beneficial activities; and
- TV and video games provide an unrealistic view of the world which emphasizes the worst characteristics of our society (violence, commercialism, sexism, etc.)

The arguments for use of television and associated media (videos, DVDs, video games), in general:
- TV and video games provide entertainment;
- TV and video games provide learning experiences, or trigger further learning, through a variety of cartoons, regular programming, public television, documentaries, and special interest channels.

Unschooling children often binge on television and video games during the deschooling process or after parents lift a restriction. Innumerable families, however, have told similar stories which result in children's binge responses leveling out over time. (The same concept applies to food restrictions and binges.)

I have never limited my children's screen time. They often go a week without turning on the televison or a few days without turning on their computers. We have never had television service. The children have seen it at other people's houses, but have never asked for it.

Arguments against computer use typically involve Internet use by young children with fear of inappropriate content, cyberbullies, or online predators cited. However, children can avoid disturbing content by using child-safe browsers, services such as a child-safe YouTube video interface (i.e., Totlol), and children's search engines. (See the Resource chapter for a list of services.)

I have chosen to provide Web access to my kids in a relatively unlimited form while still protecting their safety. Rather than use a child browser, I maintain a home web page for them, *Dragon's Fire*, with all their favorite links and new posts each day, which helps them stay within the realm of their comfort and interests. We talk about the potential dangers in the online world, what information to keep secret, and other online safety practices.

Dragon's Fire
http://dragonsfirelearning.blogspot.com

Create Your Own Homeschool Learning Blog
http://homeschool.suite101.com

Learning Experiences

As a family settles into the unschooling lifestyle, they recognize more and more of the learning that each member does during the course of regular activities. Parents gain a sense of when their children feel receptive to guidance and the introduction of new topics, and they learn to trust their children to seek out what they want or need to know. This chapter includes sections on

- Learning at home,
- Schooly supplies,
- Learning outside of home, and
- Structured classes.

Children learn something during all of their activities and restful periods, regardless of how obvious or not that something appears to others, or how valuable or not that something seems to others. In time, parents learn to recognize everyday learning, to see the value of activity and rest, and to respect the personal value of all learning.

When one of my daughters tells me that she does not feel like continuing with a project, I appreciate that she has learned to respect her own limits and take a break when she needs one. I don't want to see her pushing ahead against her healthy desire to take a break. I continue deschooling my own trained inclination to push against my natural need for rest.

Depending on differences in lifestyle, unschooling children may do more learning at home or away, through natural life experience or through more conventional educational means. In any case, when children enjoy what they spend time doing, the possibilities for growth exist in abundance. ♡

Learning at Home

We learn through doing, and many of the things we do take place at home, near home, or from home as a launching point. At home, for my family, includes our garden, the woods behind the house, the creek, the nearby playground, the river beach down the hill, the lake up the hill, and the nearby neighborhood and businesses.

Some activities a child may do at home include reading, writing, drawing, crafting, cooking, baking, cleaning and home repair, pet care, yard work and gardening, observing the sky, having conversations about anything, doing business, swimming, bike riding, imagining, etc.

Explicitly educational activities typically give clearly stated learning objectives. Some educational activities a child may do at home include taking online courses, telecourses, and correspondence courses, watching videos, listening to audiotapes, reading books and textbooks, doing workbooks, performing experiments, exploring and observing, etc.

Nonfiction Books. We can choose nonfiction books, purchased or borrowed, to help our children pursue specific interests and find answers to their questions. Depending on their age, they may prefer our active involvement in the process or simply to help them acquire the books.

Books as sources of information include textbooks, reference books, and narratives such as autobiographies and memoirs.

> Narrative books written by people who feel passion for a subject can engage and inspire readers.

Lapbooks. Basically, a lapbook includes a folder containing a collection of booklets, envelopes, pages, charts, stories, drawings, and anything else a child chooses to include.

Children can use lapbooks a variety of ways for a variety of purposes.

> Lapbooks make attractive portfolio pieces.

Lapbooks actively engage children and give them an opportunity to use craft skills and creativity.

My children have made lapbooks on topics including money, dolphins, our genealogical history, primates, environmental conservation, apples, holidays, and our town history. They keep their lapbooks in a file box and enjoy looking through them and adding to them when they learn new things.

Math. Most of us learned math in the abstract, sometimes confusing ways school teachers present it, such as through lectures, textbook reading, drilling, and testing. In this way, we relied heavily on memorization of tables and formulas and less on a conceptual understanding, which often proves difficult for kids to acquire in the school setting.

While parents typically understand how their children can learn basic math and computation skills simply through everyday activities, they may worry over the more advanced, specialized math skills, which perhaps they never mastered themselves.

Unschoolers learn advanced math as the need arises. We use math as a tool for many purposes, such as baking, building, gardening, distributing portions, and using money. An unschooling child may pursue more advanced math on the way to figuring out how to program a computer or use complicated software.

Math application includes pattern recognition, sorting, measurement, logic, problem-solving, probability, statistics, etc. Math skills help us double a recipe, build a playhouse, divide garden plots, play a board game, buy a toy, etc.

When our children wish to learn an advanced math concept that we ourselves don't understand, we need not worry. We need only to help them find the information to learn from (books, computer games, DVDs, classes, tutorials, professionals, tutors, etc.)

Reading and Writing. According to the *World Book*, children across North America typically receive reading instruction

World Book
http://worldbook.com

and begin to read on their own sometime during grade one, at about six or seven years old. This, however, does not imply that these children read with comprehension and compose works in beautiful script.

In keeping with the unschooling values of trust and respect, unschooling children learn to read and write when they decide to do so. The process of learning to read may take months or years, and it may begin at any age. Given the time and space to do so, and the freedom to find one's own preferred method, learning to read can proceed without stress.

In my family, for example, I witnessed my daughters paying attention to letters at around two or three years old, pretending to read (play reading), learning sounds between three and four years old, and sounding out and recognizing whole words from about age five onward.

My daughters learned to read from many sources. Their father and I have always alternated reading to them each night

Starfall
http://www.starfall.com

before bed, as well as at other times during the day. They have used portions of the Hooked on Phonics program, the Starfall website, the Sesame Street television series, and lessons from the book *Teach Your Child to Read in 100 Easy Lessons* by Siegfried Engelmann (Fireside, 1986).

Ilana learned to read at an earlier age than Maia before her, perhaps because our home already had learning materials and activities sprinkled about. By the time it occurred to me to offer Ilana a lesson, she already knew how to read. She had not, however, memorized the standard alphabet song.

For a child who does not express interest in reading by the age of six or seven, read to them, read to yourself, sprinkle your home with reading materials, and don't worry unnecessarily. Children will eventually want to read on their own.

> Books provide only one form of reading material. Offer magazines, comics, or video games to a child who does not feel drawn to story books.

Science. Like math, science surrounds us. Science, in general, involves observing, measuring, and thinking about what would happen if circumstances changed. Your children demonstrate their interests in scientific concepts when they play in the mud, help with baking, or ask how things work.

Before specialized vocabulary, offer tools such as microscopes, prepared slides, magnifying glasses, beakers, test tubes, tweezers, rulers, food coloring, etc., and lots of opportunity to explore.

Show your children your own curiosity about the world. Answer their questions and help them find answers to the ones you don't know (through books, classes, videos, experiments, etc.) Don't worry about scientific disciplines or terminology. Your children will pick up these labels when they persist with a topic. Focus on having fun exploring and experimenting.

Perhaps as an early sign of her fascination with all things aquatic, I remember Maia at age three telling me that she wanted to learn about "fishology." ♡

Over time, my family has created our own layered form of learning, in which we learn first in the most casual, experiential way, and later delve further and further into the complexities of the topic through various connections, forms of media, and sometimes paperwork.

History and Social Sciences. The people disciplines, history and social sciences tell stories. The history I remember from my school days emphasized facts, chronological events, dates, names, etc., all found in a reference textbook. My children have access to biographies, narratives, documentaries, docu-dramas, historical plays, and sometimes even people who remember historic events. When we travel, we take note of historical landmarks.

Don't worry about chronological order. Children feel drawn at different times to specific time periods, people, or geographic areas. The chronological context for those times and places develops as your child learns about different periods. Your children may enjoy using timelines and maps to plot events.

My daughters have a timeline of prehistory stretched across the wall next to their bunk bed and a large map of the world in the hallway outside their door.

My daughters have enjoyed learning about people and places through a monthly subscription of mystery-solving adventures, which each take place in a different part of the world, and also through a series of adventure stories covering the fifty U.S. states, as well as through Mary Pope Osborne's *Magic Tree House* series. Whenever we get a new installment or book, we create a new pile of related books in our library, and we notice when the topic comes into our lives in other ways.

Your child's historical interests may evolve from other interest areas such as art, cars, buildings, appliances, landmarks, etc. History, like other 'subjects,' connects to everything else. We need not focus on or limit ourselves to any particular subject area or course of study.

Schooly Supplies and Curricula

The key to using 'schooly,' or educational materials designed with learning in mind, lies in your children's use of them of their own choosing and for their own purposes. My daughters have used curricular programs such as Hooked on Phonics, but they use them in their own ways. They don't necessarily follow the steps or complete all the repetitions.

Likewise, I enjoy browsing lesson plans on homeschool share websites, as well as flipping through educational catalogs and websites such as

> Homeschool.com
> *http://homeschool.com*
> Large selection of educational programs.

Homeschool.com. I use these sources for ideas that I can offer to my children when I suspect they will enjoy using them.

A curriculum typically consists of lesson plans for the teacher, and textbooks, workbooks, and related supplies and materials for the students. The program may include the service of a certified teacher for management and testing. Some programs give school credit if the children complete the program according to its rules, which older unschoolers may choose to do, if for example, they want to earn a high school diploma.

Additional educational sources include

- Reference books (such as atlases, dictionaries, and encyclopedias),
- Field guides,
- Newspapers,
- Magazines,
- Library items (books, videos, CDs, and audiotapes),
- Educational computer games,
- Science equipment and kits,
- Arts and crafts kits,
- Tools and building kits, and
- Musical instruments and instruction.

Through the supply company, Fun Books, you can order unschooling-friendly curriculum guides and educational materials

on a number of topics, as well as back issues of John Holt's *Growing Without Schooling* magazine.

With stacks of educational materials around the house, you may feel like you have things covered, but look also to community resources such as libraries, museums, historical sites, courthouses, nature centers, etc., as well as people you know who can share skills, answer questions, and allow your children to observe or help them at work.

Learning Outside of Home

Many learning experiences take place away from home, in obvious places such as libraries, museums, and schools, and also through visits with friends, daily errands, trips to new places, trips to favorite places, and on and on.

Maia has a secret spot outdoors where she sits, thinks, relaxes, watches the neighborhood, and only she knows what else with time and space to herself. She often comes home with a lot to tell me. ♡

My daughters take classes, attend library events, and go to free musical and theatrical performances during the summer. They participate in clubs, activities, and science fairs with our homeschool group.

Our family makes trips to national parks and other destinations in the surrounding area. We take advantage of free ranger talks, aquarium talks, and beach naturalist talks.

We visit community gardens, nature centers, parks, wildlife preserves, zoos, pet shops, small museums, art galleries, historical society events, astronomical society events, courthouse tours, etc.

Some children volunteer in exchange for lessons or admission to museums or arts events. Some children participate in apprenticeship programs, volunteer jobs, group travel, and other opportunities.

Neighbors, friends, family, and others in the community present myriad potential sources of knowledge and experience. Parents in homeschooling groups can pool their expertise for the benefit of all the children. Learning from professionals in your community can take the form of interviews, observation, participation, lessons, an instructed course, or a mentoring relationship.

Local homeschooling groups often organize clubs and activities and share learning resources. My family has membership in several groups. Each group offers fun activities and interesting people to spend time with. Parents and children can easily start a special-interest group such as a study group, reading circle, or activity club (astronomy, geology, survival skills, writing, books, crafts, pop music, Spanish, geocaching, letterboxing, etc.)

Public school clubs, charter schools, alternative schools, and community colleges often admit homeschoolers to take individual classes. Pay special attention, however, to the requirements of attending a school. In some cases, even part-time attendance takes away homeschooling status and associated freedoms.

Structured Classes

Classes may cover interests such as theater, music, dance, gymnastics, art, sports, martial arts, foreign languages, computer programming, etc.

When looking for a class, consider your child's learning style and temperament. Private classes carry the same

> The instructor's approach and demeanor can make all the difference in a child's experience.

risks to a child's spontaneity, creativity, and love of learning as regular schooling.

When Maia at age five wanted to take a ballet class at our local performing arts center, I worried that she would not enjoy a structured class. During her first session of classes, she often acted out and didn't follow directions. Her stern instructor simply ignored her.

I wanted to pull her out of the class, but she wanted to stay. Toward the end of each class, another instructor would come in and teach a short session of tap dancing. She drew the kids in with a relaxed and upbeat approach. When it came time to sign up for the next session, I made sure to get that instructor.

The change of instructor had an immediate, positive affect on Maia's conduct. I suspect that she had acted out during the first session in an attempt to bring joy to the solemn atmosphere. ♡

Ilana wanted to learn ballet as well, but didn't want to attend classes without me, so I bought her a DVD called *Baby Ballet* (Kultur Video, 2004), and she learned as much–perhaps more–as her sister. Classes come in many forms.

> DVD classes provide another option.

Many organizations offer classes, including
- City parks and recreation districts,
- Community colleges,
- Craft stores,
- Art galleries,
- Theaters,
- Music stores,
- Museums,
- Science centers,
- Nature centers, etc.

Additional sources include private instructors, student

tutors, mentor programs, correspondence courses, online classes, etc.

My daughters have taken pony riding lessons and soccer through the city parks and recreation program, which also offers classes in arts, fitness, gardening, photography, geology, rafting, local history, languages, and much more.

Classes taken through community colleges, cooperative public schools, charter schools, and accredited private schools may offer school credit to homeschoolers for those courses completed if your child wishes to earn credit. Notice, however, the potential impact to your legal status as homeschoolers when you enroll part-time in an accredited school.

Your choices for class format may include group classes, private classes, classes for specific age groups, classes for all ages, adult classes that allow teens, etc. You may want to request a trial period to determine whether or not the class provides what your child has in mind.

Local homeschool groups can often provide listings of class opportunities in the community that admit homeschoolers. My local group's website lists business that give home educator discounts, as well as a lengthy list of classes and activities of interest to homeschoolers. The list includes volunteer opportunities, educational enrichment programs, recreation and sports, arts, dance, theater, etc. Our local public library offers a class specifically for homeschoolers to learn to use the library's resources for research, as well as study groups, book clubs, and other opportunities.

You can also browse your local yellow pages for businesses that may provide learning opportunities to your child. Besides the many businesses specifically offering classes, local professionals may submit to interviews by students, and some may have interest in mentoring.

If your child feels drawn to a particular career or career area, an interview with a professional can provide realistic information about that career and related careers. Many children know, for example, that they want to work with animals, but they may not know of the wide variety of career possibilities within that area. Mentoring, somewhat like an apprenticeship, can provide your child with realistic experience.

When chosen carefully, classes can serve as helpful sources of information and experiences relating to a child's interests, as well as provide an introduction to the institutional format of many workplaces and much of society.

Recordkeeping
and Legal Requirements

Meeting legal requirements relies heavily on record keeping. Unschooling parents may choose to keep records of their children's activities for personal or legal reasons, depending upon local regulatory requirements. This chapter includes sections on
- Measures of learning,
- Meeting legal requirements,
- Recordkeeping methods, and
- Preparing for tests and evaluations.

Some parents enjoy keeping records, some don't, and some do it only in order to meet legal requirements. Records can serve as keepsakes for personal recollection, as well as for reference for future college and job applications. They can take numerous forms, including journals, portfolios, charts, and fill-in forms.

Each record keeping strategy carries strengths and weaknesses and can serve different purposes. Some parents purchase record keeping systems while others choose to create their own. Whatever method you use, I recommend keeping records mostly to yourself, especially with young children, so they don't feel measured.

Taking Measure of Learning

Unschooling parents typically take an active interest in their children's activities. They don't need grades or tests to show them which skills their children have demonstrated. Nonetheless, some parents document their children's learning activities.

Some localities enforce legal requirements for testing and filing of official forms. Some areas allow parents the choice of testing, presenting a portfolio, or writing up reports.

Conventional styles of homeschooling lend themselves more easily to record keeping, whereas unschooling typically requires more creativity in fitting learning experiences into subject categories. However, families of all styles have found ways to satisfy record keeping requirements.

Perhaps the simplest way to record an unschooler's learning activities involves periodically listing what the child has spent time doing, i.e., reading, making, watching, listening to, visiting, talking about, etc.

I publish a spiral-bound journal, *Recordkeeping for Unschoolers*, with prompts, information, and inspirational tips based on that simple concept.

Recordkeeping for Unschoolers, a spiral-bound journal available through *UnschoolingLifestyle.com*

My own record keeping practice has changed over the years. My local government requires homeschool registration, record keeping, and annual testing to correspond with the school year when a child turns eight years old and each year thereafter.

During my children's early years, I kept a monthly list of things they had done or talked about. I kept drawings and other art projects in a treasure box (still do.)

I knew very well that Maia, at age 3, felt especially drawn to animals, especially dinosaurs, and that she could name and imitate hundreds of them. I knew that she learned through books, videos, trips to the pet store, zoos, and fairs. I learned, through the practice of recording Maia's activities, that she learned far more than I may have otherwise consciously noticed, which bolstered my confidence in unschooling.

As children grow older and more independent in their activities, they can take some of the responsibility for keeping records of their interests and activities. Some parents ask their older homeschoolers to keep a journal of the books they read, the activities they do, and anything else they wish to record.

Meeting Legal Requirements

Most localities have compulsory schooling laws, so new unschooling families will want to learn how homeschooling, in general, fits within those laws and what specifically the local government requires. Note that homeschoolers and school children may have different academic learning requirements.

I recommend against identifying yourself as unschoolers to regulators. To avoid evoking fear or criticism, you might describe your children as homeschoolers who follow a custom curriculum.

Homeschooling regulations, such as learning requirements and testing, don't resonate with unschooling philosophy, so parents may struggle to reconcile feelings of annoyance or injustice with the acknowledgment that they must meet legal requirements in order to continue homeschooling. Principles and ideals feel wonderful, but we want to seriously consider the consequences for honoring them, such as revocation of our granted-freedom to homeschool.

Seek legal information from a variety of sources, rather than relying on, for example, school officials who may know little about homeschooling or may provide discouraging answers based on the fact that schools rely on student attendance for funding.

Homeschool Legal Defense Association
http://www.hslda.org
Information on laws and litigation. (Note: Christian organization.)

In some areas, local laws don't explicitly authorize homeschooling, yet people can homeschool by registering a home, church, or other group as a private school, or by some other trick.

A local homeschooling group offers perhaps the most reliable source of information about homeschooling regulations. Experienced homeschoolers can tell you not only what the law says, but also how local government enforces it. For example, my state requires annual testing by a certified teacher, and we must keep record of it, but we need not turn in test results. In addition, several local certified teachers offer an unschooler-friendly "no test" test.

Your local government might require you to do the following.

- Fill out and file forms such as a *Declaration of Intent to Homeschool*;
- Register your home as a private school;
- Submit an education plan or curriculum; or
- Record attendance (school days) and complete a specified number of days per year.

Through creativity, you can fit your child's learning experiences into such forms. Unschooling parent, Carol Narigon, created a sample 'Unschooling Curriculum' to serve as a model.

> Carol Narigon's
> Unschooling Curriculum
> *http://www.sandradodd.com/*
> *unschoolingcurriculum.html*

An unschooling curriculum lists the subjects you and your child expect to cover. In other words, explain what you and your child will probably do over the course of the school year, using your government's requirements and *WorldBook* as a guide.

I know my daughters' interests and I expect we will continue to seek out related activities.

Unintentionally, through 'standards-based' online game subscriptions (BrainPOP, JumpStart, KidzClix), my children already cover the basic requirements.

BrainPOP
http://www.brainpop.com

JumpStart
http://www.jumpstart.com

KidzClix
http://www.kidzclix.net

If my local government did require me to submit an education plan, I would take the unschooling curriculum a step further and list probable activities under the standard subject headings of

- Social Studies,
- Science,
- Language Arts,
- Health,
- Mathematics, and
- The Arts.

I may list LEGO club under Mathematics, gardening and baking under Science, and Spanish club under both Social Studies and Language Arts. Etc. Use your creativity.

If homeschooling regulations feel unjust, join together with other homeschoolers and

History of Education System
http://www.quantumshift.tv

work to change the laws. I believe that a day will come when unschooling has proven its merit to a majority of people. The school system has not existed for long in the human timeline. Things can change.

Recordkeeping Methods

Methods for keeping records of your child's learning activities include

- Journaling,
- Blogging,
- Assembling portfolios,
- Creating charts, and
- Filling out forms.

Journals. Historically, a person added to a narrative journal at the end of each day (i.e., a journey takes a day), but you can jot down notes weekly, monthly, or quarterly. Either you or your child, or both, can keep a journal. The journal may contain lists of activities, descriptions of trips taken, specific learning observed, etc. You can later take the information from a journal and transfer it to a portfolio or to forms, as necessary.

Some parents write in their journals at the end of each day, noting every observable activity. Other parents write less frequently, taking note of prominent activities and interests. I made more frequent notes during my children's younger years when they added major abilities every day. Nowadays, their projects span longer periods of time.

Blogs. A blog, short for web log, works like a journal. You can keep it private or post it for the world to see.

My children's home page and blog, *Dragon's Fire*, serves primarily as 'online sprinkling' for them (i.e., a trail to follow if they wish), but also as a method of recordkeeping for me. I date and label each post with an official subject category so I can easily click a category and see what my children had exposure to during specific time periods. In addition, I keep a family blog for sharing our goings on with long-distance family and friends.

Create Your Own Homeschool Learning Blog
http://homeschool.suite101.com

Portfolios. You can collect samples of your children's

work (i.e., artistic product, calculation scratch paper, journal pages, etc.) and assemble it into a portfolio. A portfolio may take the form of a scrapbook, filing cabinet, box, or some combination that allows you to showcase your child's knowledge of academic requirements, as well as other interests. The portfolio may contain written reports, workbook pages, lists of books read, journal notes about various activities, artwork, videotapes, photos, or anything else. To prepare your child's portfolio for assessment, choose pieces that show specific learning achievements as referenced in your local homeschool learning requirements.

Charts. You can create a chart, or grid, divided into subject categories with lists of learning activities. The chart may list academic subjects along one axis and days of the week along the other. List activities under as many categories as may apply. For example, building with LEGOs could fall under Mathematics and Art/Social Studies, and learning Spanish could fall under Language Arts and Social Studies. You could call Spanish a unit study that spans many categories.

Forms. Some school districts provide official forms on which to fill in coverage of learning requirements. Some districts may accept common language to describe learning activities, whereas others prefer the use of educational jargon. For example, reading a book for hours may be called 'uninterrupted, silent, sustained reading.'

Child-led, interest-driven activities that cover multiple categories could translate as 'interdisciplinary unit studies using learner-initiated activities,' or as 'project learning,' or 'block learning.'

Years of homeschool records may come in handy for use in preparing a transcript for submission to a school, military, or

Mary Griffith
http://marygriffith.net

workplace. As with other traditional forms, you may have to use creativity to present an unschooler's education in such a manner. Mary Griffith provides an example of an unschooler's transcript in her book, *The Unschooler's Handbook* (Prima, 1998). Alternatively, you can present a portfolio in place of a transcript.

Preparing for Tests and Evaluations

Your local government may require
* Standardized testing,
* Portfolio assessment,
* Performance assessment, or
* Progress reports.

Check with a local homeschool group or with your local school district for specific requirements. You may find a summary of your area's legal requirements at the websites of the

> HSLDA
> *http://hslda.org*
>
> U.S. Dept. of Education
> *http://www.ed.gov*

Homeschool Legal Defense Association (HSLDA) or your local government's department or ministry of education website.

Standardized Testing. If your locality requires standardized testing, you can ask for a copy of a previous edition of the test so that you and your children can go over it and practice it. You can attempt to negotiate a new test or type of assessment if you feel that the test shows a bias against your educational philosophy.

Your local government may require testing as often as annually or less often. Some governments require testing only near the end of specific school years such as grade levels 3,5,8, and 10. School districts typically supply, administer, and pay for testing, however, parents may have the option to hire an independent tester. Ask local homeschool groups and associations to refer unschooler-friendly testers. You may find a mail-in test that you and your child can do together at home.

Homeschoolers typically outperform publicly schooled children on standardized tests. At the time of this publishing, homeschoolers

> Homeschool students typically test at or above the 85th percentile.

in my country outperformed their public school peers by 37 percent [Dr. Brian Ray. *Progress Report 2009: Homeschool Academic Achievement and Demographics*. National Home Education Research Institute (NHERI), 2009].

Portfolio Assessment. As an alternative to standardized testing, some local governments accept submission of a portfolio. In this case, you and your child would assemble a selection of work samples or other presentation that showcases your child's learning achievements. Portfolio items might include written reports by people who have worked with your child, video or audio tapes, photographs, relevant newspaper clippings, brochures from places visited, lists of books read, etc.

Performance Assessment. In this case, your child might submit to an interview or perform tasks that show mastery of required subjects. These tasks might include presentations on activities or projects such as theatrical performances, written reports, or science projects.

Progress Reports. In lieu of testing, your locality may require you to file periodic progress reports, consisting of descriptions of your children's learning activities over a specified period of time, such as a quarter, semester, or school year. Information from a journal helps you to easily create this type of report.

Sample Recordkeeping for Unschoolers
Maia, December - February

Doing: Pop Bottle Science experiments, Faunasphere.com, Poptropica.com missions, JumpStart Virtual World tasks, ballet class, Spanish club, gymnastics

Making: 3D wooden puzzle of T-rex, simple machine constructions with physics kit, *LEGO Crazy Action Contraptions* (Klutz, 2008), LEGO robotics, hand-made paper dolls, drawings

Reading: *Wright on Time, Magic Tree House* #29, *Avalon* book 2, *Harry Potter* series, *Eragon*; jokes and riddles, *Alice in Wonderland*

Writing: Story about a princess, poems, songs; cursive script, keyboarding, Kanji

Watching: Dr. Who, Primeval, Christmas movies, Johnny Test, Animated Hero Classics, Magic School Bus

Listening: Audiobook fairytales, pop music, reggae, Christmas music; French instruction CD

Talking: Megalodon, shark-men mythology, dolphins, Barbie animal trainer, makeup, punk style clothing, hairstyles, California and Arizona

Planning: Overnight train trip, upcoming lunar eclips, telescope, Galileo video

Visiting: Marine theme park to see dolphins

Sample Unschooler Curriculum
3rd Grade Level

Social Studies: We plan to explore holidays, folk customs, and cultures around the world, Native American and U.S. history, The Story of Stuff (*http://storyofstuff.org*), local and world geography, maps, and orienteering.

Science: We plan to study animal and plant wildlife, prehistoric life, life cycles, habitats, conservation, climate change, electricity and magnetism, outer space and spacecrafts, solar and lunar cycles, machines, and the scientific method.

Language Arts: We plan to read fiction and nonfiction, prose and poetry, use the dictionary, note alphabetization and spelling, compose written works, and use print, cursive script, keyboarding, and punctuation.

Health: We plan to practice good hygiene and online safety, eat healthful foods, study anatomical systems, engage in physical activity, dress for the weather, and apply first aid when necessary.

Math: We plan to build, measure, experiment, bake, sew, divide, add and subtract, estimate, figure math puzzles, make charts and graphs, discuss the concept of negative numbers, compare measurement and numeric systems, and keep track of time.

Arts: We plan to attend dance and art classes, make arts and crafts at home, compose written works, act out plays, and take photos.

An Unschooling Course of Study
on El Día de los Muertos

The following course of events illustrates how my children and I enjoyed the subject of Halloween and El Día de los Muertos.

"Mictecacihuatl, Queen of Mictlan, the underworld, keeps watch over the bones of the dead. The Lady of the Dead presides over El Día de los Muertos, the festival to honor ancestors. Some people believe that this time of year, the ninth month of the Aztec calendar, allows easier access for souls to visit the living. Some families set up altars with memorial objects and offerings for their beloved ancestors."~from Dragon's Fire: *Aztec Day of the Dead*

- *Top Secret Adventures, Case #32751, The Mystery South of the Border* (Highlights.com), arrived in the mail.
- Each morning my eldest daughter consults her calendar and counts down the days til Halloween.
- My daughters and I attended Spanish Club, an activity of our local homeschool group, where we learned a bit about the Day of the Dead, and then made sugar skulls, papel picado, and calavera masks.
- We checked out a stack of library books about Halloween, Day of the Dead, Aztecs, Trick-or-Treating, etc.
- We went to a pumpkin patch and watched *It's the Great Pumpkin, Charlie Brown* (Warner, 1966).
- I searched the Web for more Halloween and Día de los Muertos activities and my daughters and I decorated our house with them.
- We unpacked last year's Halloween decorations and put them up.
- I created a Day of the Dead post on my daughters' learning blog from which they begin each Internet

session.

- We watched a BrainPOP.com video about Spanish and Mexico, which mentioned Day of the Dead.
- We read *The Search for the Missing Bones, The Magic School Bus, Chapter Book No. 2* (Scholastic, 2000) about skeletons and Halloween, and also began a human anatomy science kit, *Journey Into the Human Body, The Magic School Bus Young Scientist Club*.
- We put up a large poster of a skeleton, labeled the bones, and located the same bones within our bodies.
- We listened to spooky music and discussed the differences between scary Halloween and joyful Day of the Dead.

And we had just begun...

A Sample Learning Topic Narrative

My daughter, Maia, feels especially drawn to marine life and the water world. She wants to study, help protect, train, and otherwise work with marine mammals. We have made numerous trips to the local aquarium where she plans to apply for the teen volunteer apprenticeship program. In the meantime, she can attend aquarium classes and camps for younger children, as well as seek out other opportunities toward her goal.

She spends time along the shores. Maia gently touches sea stars, urchins, and anemones. She holds crabs and snails in her hands and once stood in awe over the washed up remains of a shark. We visit aquariums and marine parks when we travel.

Maia's interest in marine life has led her to watch documentaries about biologists, divers, film-makers, aquariums around the world, whales and dolphins, ancient ocean life, the plight of coral reefs, etc. She studies marine life in encyclopedias and collects figures of marine mammals and amphibians.

Her interest, which began with marine mammals, has grown to include ocean habitats, plant life, fish and sharks, shore birds, animal training, diving, tide pools, islands, weather, magnetism, and on and on.

Along this course, Maia and her sister have watched a television series about mermaids in which the antagonist marine biologist's scientific curiosity has caused her to lose sight of the natural rights of ocean life. Even the title of the show, *H2O: Just Add Water* (Jonathan M. Shiff, Film Finance, 2006), inspired Maia's interest in chemical formulas, which led to numerous pop-bottle science experiments.

College and Career

Homeschoolers who plan to attend college typically apply with their own transcript or portfolio or through an official modified admissions process. This chapter includes sections on

- The teen years,
- College and career prospects,
- Adapting to institutional environments, and
- Alternatives to college.

Unschoolers don't have grade point averages, school transcripts, or diplomas to present for college admission. However, many, if not most, colleges accept homeschool transcripts and provide a modified admissions process for students who come from non-traditional school backgrounds.

Nonetheless, some parents worry about their unschooling child's transition from pressure-free learning experiences to college assignments, deadlines, grades, and testing.

Unschoolers may or may not have experience with the traditional teaching model, but they do have resourcefulness and the ability to take responsibility for their own learning, which will serve them well in the realm of college and career.

The Teen Years

An unschooler may spend the teen years in much the same way as earlier years with self-motivated, self-directed activities, which may extend to include career-focused internships, apprenticeships, volunteer job positions, or college courses.

The idea of high school in the minds of former high school students, such as myself and many unschooling parents, may conjure various 'advanced' subject categories–calculus, physics, etc.–the ones some parents fear they cannot help their children to learn. Firstly, a teenager who wants to learn these subjects can find a way to do so. Secondly, advanced subjects have their place, which may or may not fit with your teen's idea of meaningful life work. In addition, not all high school students take advanced classes.

During my early teen years, I thought I wanted to do accounting work. With that in mind, I took every math class available...until the day my grandma took me to meet her accountant. I went prepared with a list of questions about the job. I came away with a much different image than the one I had held. If I had not met a real-life accountant, I may have kept taking math and accounting classes throughout college.

I took away from those high school years, not so much the subjects covered as the restlessness and sense of "doing time" until my release into the adult world. High school busywork inhibited my search for meaningful life work. My impatience won out when I left high school before finishing my time.

Unschoolers, on the other hand, have the freedom to move in a direct line toward their goals. If an unschooling teen has not already found meaningful life work, the learning activities may center around exploring careers, talking with people about their work, developing mentoring relationships, networking and making connections with people in fields of interest, doing volunteer jobs, etc.

My state offers a dual-enrollment program called Running Start, which provides up to two years of tuition-free college classes for high school

> Running Start
> *http://k12.wa.us/*
> *runningstart*

juniors and seniors. College-bound unschoolers can take advantage of this benefit. Similar programs may exist in other localities. However, like homeschooler outreach programs, pay close attention to participation requirements.

College and Career Prospects

Unschoolers who plan to attend college may want to familiarize themselves some time in advance with homeschool-specific admissions policies, as well as with scholarships, grants, and financial aid application processes.

The college application process typically includes placement testing and submission of a transcript or portfolio and perhaps recommendation letters, essays, and financial records.

Testing. Some colleges require prospective students to pass standardized tests such as the SAT, PSAT, and ACT tests, as well as college placement tests. Unschoolers can prepare for these tests by using one of many available test preparation books or online courses. Some public libraries offer test preparation workshops or tutoring.

Transcript. In addition to testing, colleges may require homeschoolers to prepare their own transcripts, or otherwise summarize what they have learned that demonstrates their preparedness to take

> For a sample transcript, search the Internet for 'high school transcript sample' or 'homeschool transcript template.'

college-level courses. A transcript lists the standard high school subjects pre-required for firs-year college students (i.e., a list of learning activities and experiences translated into standard course names), along with the equivalent of grades and credit hours for each subject.

Community College. Some teen unschoolers demonstrate their college readiness by taking courses at a local community college or technical school, perhaps through a high school dual-enrollment program. Some community colleges and technical schools offer transfer programs, such as 'liberal studies,' in which students can take many of their undergraduate requirements for less cost than at a larger college. This option may give unschoolers easier entrance into a university.

Community college courses also give unschoolers the experience, if they have never had it, of sitting in a classroom and complying with schedules and expectations, as well as interacting with fellow students who don't necessarily value learning for its own sake.

Adapting to Institutional Environments

Unschoolers have years of experience taking personal responsibility for their learning, as well as for making other decisions in their lives. They carry the benefit of this experience with them into institutions such as colleges and workplaces.

College-bound unschoolers often begin taking college courses at earlier ages than their public school peers, and thus already know what to expect. Unschoolers who begin college in their middle teens may feel less urgency to hurry through college and can take their time to get comfortable with college routines.

Unschoolers typically enjoy learning. For this reason, they may have difficulty understanding college peers who devise shortcuts and alternatives to learning that allow them to simply pass tests and courses.

An unschooler's natural curiosity and love of learning colors the experience of college and work life.

- Unschoolers use their creativity to find enjoyable ways to learn the required subject material.
- Unschoolers know how to find alternative sources of information and experience, in addition to the sources assigned by instructors.
- Unschoolers feel comfortable taking responsibility and making important decisions.

Regardless of whether or not business owners or employees hold a degree, they still have to learn on the job in order to do the work. Employers know this, which can work in a resourceful unschooler's favor. Unschoolers have always taken responsibility for their own learning. They know how to solve problems on their own, when to ask for help, and where to find that help. Their love of learning, and lack of a learned dislike of assigned work, aid them in college and career success.

Alternatives to College

John Holt said, "If you know what kind of work you want to do, move toward it in the most direct way possible. If you want someday to build boats, go where people are building boats, find out as much as you can."

College provides one way, not necessarily the best way, for your child to prepare for meaningful life work. Apprenticeships and internships may provide an easier and

> Why Work?
> *http://whywork.org*
> Unjobbing: Alternatives to traditional employment.

potentially optimal path to a rewarding career. Participating in a mentoring relationship may mark the first step your child takes toward exploring a prospective career.

Independent-study programs, correspondence courses, apprenticeships, internships, volunteer jobs, etc., all can serve as pathways to finding meaningful work. Opportunities abound for learning about the things one wants to know about. We learn most effectively by doing.

Unschoolers who have made their own way into the adult world of work can bring a resume of work experience rather than a college degree to their job interviews. A history of volunteer job positions, mentor relationships, and apprenticeships will stand out from those of recent college graduates.

Some college graduates discover, only after spending years

of their time and thousands of dollars, that they could have followed an easier path to get where they got, or worse, that they feel dissatisfied upon discovering the reality of their chosen career.

Conversely, unschoolers who try out jobs of interest through volunteer positions can avoid such disillusionment. Real work experiences allow unschoolers to find the work that calls to them and to do it.

A Multitude of Resources

Homeschooling resources exist in abundance and continue to grow with the rapidly increasing population of homeschoolers. This final chapter includes a listing of
- Unschooling websites,
- Homeschooling websites,
- Educational websites for children,
- Open-source learning websites,
- Sources of free stuff,
- Educational supplies and services,
- Homeschool associations and groups,
- Unschooling conferences, and
- Sources of legal information.

Unschooling-Specific Websites

The following includes unschooling-specific websites and online publications.

Unschooling America
http://unschoolingamerica.com
'Freedom to learn with liberty and justice for all.'

Théatre du Monde
http://danielleconger.organiclearning.org/unschooling.html
'...where living in the world is learning!'

Connections ezine
http://connections.organiclearning.org
Ezine of unschooling and mindful parenting.

Sandra Dodd
http://www.sandradodd.com
Always learning.

Joyfully Rejoycing
http://joyfullyrejoycing.com
Unschooling, peaceful parenting, and living joyful family lives.

Do Life Right
http://www.doliferight.com
Unschooling, healthy living, mindful parenting.

John Holt and Growing Without Schooling
http://www.holtgws.com
Continuing the work of John Holt.

Growing Without Schooling
http://www.unschooling.com/gws
Archives of John Holt's magazine.

The Natural Child Project
http://www.naturalchild.org/articles/learning.html
Articles on learning and living with children.

Life Without School
http://lifewithoutschool.typepad.com
An online publication and blogging community.

Life Learning Magazine
http://www.lifelearningmagazine.com
'Personalized, non-coercive, interest-led learning from life.'

Homeschooling Websites

The following includes some of my favorite general

homeschooling websites.

Learn in Freedom
http://learninfreedom.org
'Taking responsibility for your own learning.'

Home Education Magazine
http://www.homeedmag.com
Articles and resources with a focus on unschooling.

Homeschool.com
http://www.homeschool.com
Many articles and resources.

A to Z Home's Cool
http://homeschooling.gomilpitas.com
Lesson ideas, resources, and articles.

Best Homeschooling
http://www.besthomeschooling.org
'The best advice of seasoned homeschoolers and other educators.'

National Home Education Research Institute
http://www.nheri.org
Research and information.

Fun Educational Websites for Children

The following include a few of mine and my children's favorite, mostly free, kids' websites.

CBeebies
http://www.bbc.co.uk/cbeebies
BBC children's games, stories, and activities.

Cyberchase
http://pbskids.org/cyberchase
Math games and activities.

League of Scientists
http://www.theleagueofscientists.com
Science games.

PBS Island
http://pbskids.org/read
'Raising readers.'

PBS Kids Go!
http://pbskids.org/go
Online games.

PBS Kids Sprout
http://www.sproutonline.com
Preschool games and activities.

Poptropica
http://www.poptropica.com
Task completing adventure game.

Poisson Rouge
http://www.poissonrouge.com
Preschool games.

Planet Orange
http://orangekids.com
Financial literacy.

Sesame Street
http://www.sesamestreet.org
Preschool and early education games and videos.

Starfall
http://www.starfall.com
'Learn to read.'

Totlol
http://www.totlol.com
An inexpensive subscription to a kid-safe, community-moderated YouTube video interface.

...and many, many more. Check out our learning blog for more favorite kids' websites.

> Dragon's Fire Learning
> *http://dragonsfirelearning.blogspot.com*
> Maia, Ilana, and Kalea's blog of interests and links. ♡

Open-Source Learning Communities

The following websites host free online courses.

Wikispaces for Educators
http://www.wikispaces.com
Create your own wikis or work collaboratively with other students and homeschoolers.

Connexions
http://cnx.org
Share expertise and experience in the form of online courses.

Khan Academy
http://www.khanacademy.org
Providing a world-class education to anyone, anywhere.

Wikiversity
http://en.wikiversity.org
Set learning free, preschool to university.

MIT Open Courseware
http://ocw.mit.edu/OcwWeb/web
Free courses, lecture notes, exams, and videos from the
Massachusetts Institute of Technology.

Homeschool Launch
http://www.hslaunch.com
Share homeschooling resources.

Homeschool Share
http://www.homeschoolshare.com
Share lapbook templates, unit studies, lesson plans, etc.

Homeschool Helper
http://www.homeschoolhelperonline.com
Share unit studies ideas and plans, lapbooks, worksheets,
coloring pages, etc.

Free Stuff

Unschoolers, especially, specialize in taking advantage of free
resources. Why buy what you can get for free and meet people
in the process?

When I participated regularly in Freecycle, I met people
with interests similar to mine. When my family prepared to
move from one house to another, Freecyclers came and
gratefully took away unwanted big, heavy desks and couches.
Need something? Post a Wanted.

Freecycle
http://www.freecycle.org
Offer and request items of all kinds for no charge among local

community members.

Paperback Swap
http://www.paperbackswap.com
Trade paperback books via mail for the cost of shipping.

Couch Surfing
http://www.couchsurfing.org
For the adventurous, host your couch to travelers and stay on
other people's couches when you travel.

Educational Supplies and Services

The following include a few of my favorite homeschooling
services and supply companies.

FUN Books
http://fun-books.com
Unschooling-oriented books, games, and other materials.

Homeschool Buyer's Co-op
http://www.homeschoolbuyersco-op.org/?source=21877
Participate in group buys and save money.

Edify at Home
http://www.edifyathome.com
Online auctions for homeschooling families.

eBay
http://www.edifyathome.com
Buy and sell online auctions.

Useborne
http://www.usbornebooksandmore.com
Children's books of all kinds.

Timberdoodle
http://www.timberdoodle.com
Family-owned homeschool supply company.

Brainwaves Toys
http://www.brainwavestoys.com
Educational toys and kits.

Budget Art Kids
http://budgetartkids.com
'Jump into art, jump into fun!'

Discount Dance Supply
http://discountdance.com
'Great dance clothes at great prices.'

Remo Percussion
http://www.remo.com
Professional-quality children's instruments.

LEGO Education
http://legoeducation.us
Hands-on math, science, and technology.

Homeschool Associations and Groups

A homeschooling group, particularly one that emphasizes unschooling, can provide a valuable source of support, especially to a family that does not otherwise know any homeschoolers or whose family does not support them. If your local group does not meet your needs, consider starting your own.

Support groups may organize field trips, activities, clubs, and discussion groups for homeschooling children as well as their parents. National, regional, and local groups exist to provide different services. Some groups operate only online while others get together to form local homeschooling communities. Larger homeschool associations often list directories of regional groups.

Family Unschoolers Network
http://www.unschooling.org
Support for unschooling, homeschooling, and self-directed learning.

American Homeschool Association
http://www.americanhomeschoolassociation.org
Advocacy, support, information, and networking.

Home School Legal Defense Association
http://www.hslda.org
Advocacy, legal information, and news about legislation and legal cases.

The Canadian Homeschool Resource Page
http://www.flora.org/homeschool-ca
Information, resources, support, projects and events, laws and regulations.

Unschooling Conferences

Conferences typically provide speakers, workshops, and fun activities for the whole family.

Rethinking Education
http://www.rethinkingeducation.net
'Rethink everything. Grow. Share. Love. Revolutionize your life.'

LIFE is Good
http://www.lifeisgoodconference.com
'Learning In Freedom Everyday.'

Good Vibrations
http://goodvibrationsconference.com
'Inspire, discuss, play, and spread lots of bubbly energy...'

The UnConvention
http://unconvention.info
'Challenge, educate, and enrich people's lives.'

Enjoy Life
http://enjoylifeunschooling.com
Presentations, funshops, chats and community events.

Great Big Happy Life
http://www.greatbighappylife.com
'Connect with like-minded families, expand your notion of what it means to live with children, and participate in the unschooling movement as it changes the world.'

Unschoolers Winter Waterpark Gathering
http://www.ugo.unschoolgathering.com
Discussions, funshops, presentations, etc., at America's largest indoor waterpark.

Unschooling Adventure Cruises
http://www.unschoolingadventurecruise.blogspot.com
'A conference on the seas for unschooling families.'

Not Back to School Camp
http://nbtsc.org
A gathering for unschooled teenagers.

Laws and Regulations

Most governments allow homeschooling. Homeschool associations typically provide the most reliable sources of information about local homeschooling laws. To locate government sources, search for 'Department of Education' in the U.S. or 'Ministry of Education' in Canada.

Home School Legal Defense Association
http://www.hslda.org
International, national, and regional advocacy, legal information, and news about legislation and legal cases.

U.S. Department of Education
http://www.ed.gov

Bookshelf

I recommend the following books on the topics of
* Unschooling,
* Parenting, and
* Nature-based learning.

Unschooling and Learning

Just some of the many books on unschooling and personally-motivated learning:

Dodd, Sandra. *Sandra Dodd's Big Book of Unschooling*, Lulu, 2009.

Dodd, Sandra. *Moving a Puddle, and other essays*. Lulu, 2005.

Fitzenreiter, Valerie. *The Unprocessed Child: Living Without School*. Unbounded Publications, 2003.

Gatto, John Taylor. *Dumbing Us Down*. New Society, 1992.

Griffith, Mary. *The Unschooling Handbook: How to Use the Whole World as Your Child's Classroom*. Prima, 1998.

Hern, Matt. *Deschooling Our Lives*. New Society, 1998.

Holt, John Caldwell; Farenga, Patrick. *Teach Your Own*. Perseus Books, 2003.

Holt, John Caldwell. *Learning All the Time*. Da Capo Press, 1989.

Jensen, Derrick. *Walking on Water: Reading, Writing, and Revolution*. Chelsea Green Publishing, 2005.

Kream, Rue. *Parenting a Free Child: An Unschooled Life*. Rue Kream, 2005.

Llewellyn, Grace. *The Teenage Liberation Handbook*. Lowry House, 1998.

Martin, Dayna. *Radical Unschooling: A Revolution Has Begun*. Tasora Books, 2009.

Prieznitz, Wendy; Aldort, Naomi; Martin, Dayna; et al. *Life Learning: Lessons from the Educational Frontier*. The Alternate Press, 2009.

Sheffer, Susannah. *A Life Worth Living: Selected Letters of John Holt*. Ohio State University Press, 1991.

Takahashi, Tammy. *Deschooling Gently*. Hunt Press, 2008.

Van Gestal, Nanda; Hunt, Jan; Quinn, Daniel; et al. *The Unschooling Unmanual*. The Natural Child Project, 2008.

Parenting

Aron, Elaine, Ph.D., *The Highly Sensitive Child*. Random House, 2002.

Cook, Julie, *Unvaccinated, Homeschooled, and TV-Free: It's Not Just for Fanatics and Zealots*. No Regrets Publishing, 2010.

Faber, Adele; Mazlish, Elaine. *Siblings Without Rivalry*. Avon Books, 1998.

Kohn, Alfie. *Unconditional Parenting: Moving from Rewards and Punishments to Love and Reason*. Atria Books, 2005.

Kurcinka, Mary Sheedy. *Raising Your Spirited Child: A Guide for Parents Whose Child is More Intense, Sensitive, Perceptive, Persistent, and Energetic*. Harper, 2006.

Liedloff, Jean. *The Continuum Concept: In Search of Happiness Lost*. Perseus Books, 1977.

Neufeld, Gordon; Mate, Gabor. *Hold On to Your Kids: Why Parents Need to Matter More Than Peers*. Ballantine Books, 2005.

Noelle, Scott. *The Daily Groove: A Creative Parents' Guide to the Art of Attraction Parenting*. Scott Noelle, 2009.

Pearce, Joseph Chilton. *Magical Child*. Plume, 1977.

Sears, William; Sears, Martha. *The Attachment Parenting Book*. Little, Brown and Company, 2001.

Small, Meredith. *Kids: How Biology and Culture Shape the Way We Raise Young Children*. Anchor Books, 2001.

Nature-Based Learning

Louv, Richard. *Last Child in the Woods: Saving Our Children from Nature-Deficit Disorder*. Algonquin Books, 2005.

Young, Jon; Haas, Ellen; and McGown, Evan. *Coyote's Guide to Connecting with Nature*. OWLink Media, 2008.

❀

This completes your introduction to a life without school. Follow your dreams and make of it what you desire. I wish you the best, most happy, fulfilling family life.

Farewell & Happy Not-Back-To-School,

Sara McGrath
Duvall, Washington
September 2010

About the Author

Sara McGrath lives in a small town outside of Seattle. She spends time exploring the area and caring for three unschooling daughters, two felines, a husband, and a small garden, as well as writing for various online and print publications.

The new book is out!

The Unschooling Happiness Project
A Guide to Living a Happy and Fulfilling Life Through Love and Creativity

The Unschooling Happiness Project
http://unschoolinglifestyle.com

Made in the USA
Lexington, KY
07 May 2014